The Prophetical Arithmology
of Daniel the Prophet

by

Harold R. Ingle

DORRANCE PUBLISHING CO., INC.
PITTSBURGH, PENNSYLVANIA 15222

Dorrance Publishing Co., Inc.
701 Smithfield Street
Pittsburgh, PA 15222
Visit our website at *www.dorrancebookstore.com*

ISBN: 978-1-4349-1209-1
eISBN: 978-1-4349-3918-0

To the reader open to the possibility that matter is an adamantine illusion.

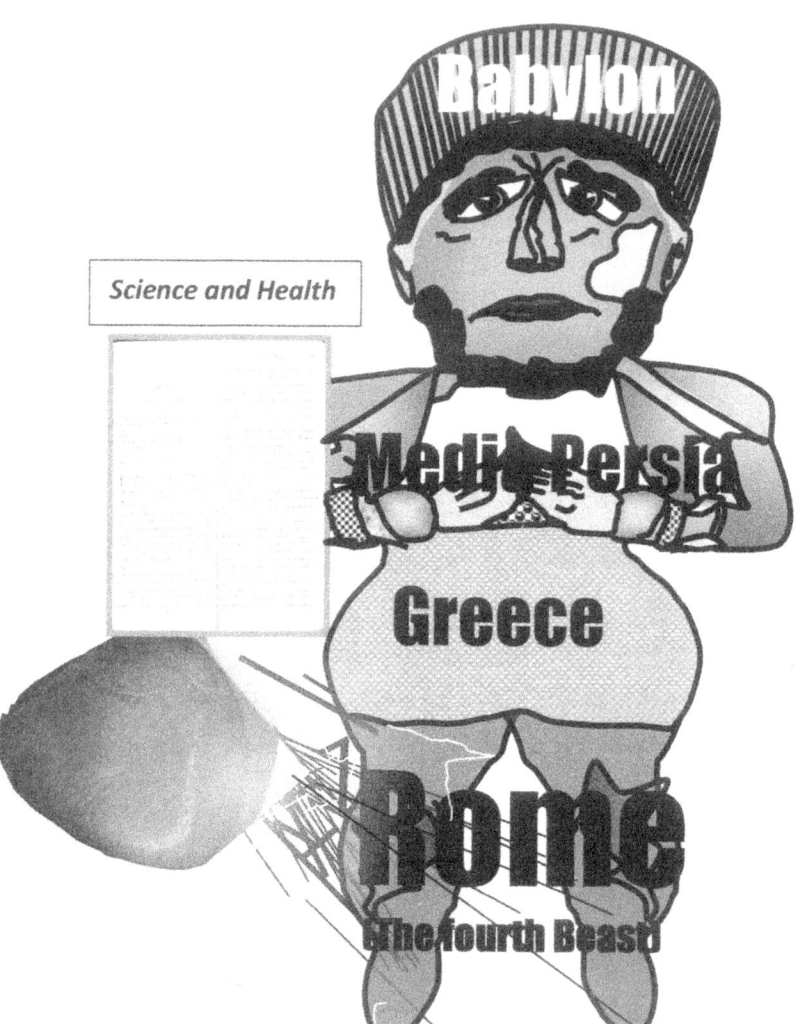

Introductory Symbolism

Figure 1 is entitled *The Four-Beast Man*. This figure embodied the political world history before the time of Daniel's periods of *abomination of desolation* concerning which this work is all about. The historical period of Jesus of Nazareth had not yet appeared. Daniel actually prophesied, quite accurately, the period of Jesus. History has so confirmed this. The writer has, somewhat arbitrarily, chosen the date of circa 606 for Daniel's prophecy writing period—although, due to his youth, it was probably ten or fifteen years later.

This is approximately one hundred years after the date the northern tribes of Israel were taken captive by the Assyrian king Shalmanesser, who put an end to the known whereabouts of Israeli tribes except for Daniel's tribe of Judah and a half-tribe of Benjamin. Jesus evidently knew where they were, for he sent his disciples to them. Daniel descended from Davidic royalty and was actually taken prisoner by the Babylonians about the year 606 or 607 B.C.

An interesting feature of Daniel's creature, represented by figure 1, is that it is top-heavy. Gold is heavier than silver. Silver is heavier than brass or bronze. Brass is heavier than iron. Iron is heavier than iron mixed with clay. The whole pagan world was top-heavy simply because it did not have God to hold it up! At the end of the abomination periods of Daniel, this condition would begin to change.

Figure 2 represents Daniel's description of the fourth beast. This beast would be the mighty Roman Empire as it evolved from a political state into an ecclesiastical state. Daniel refers to the ecclesiastical form as the period of the *little horn*. "Horn" in the Scripture represents power. The stomping feet, iron teeth, and glaring eyes show that none of the old character of the political Roman Empire was to change when it assumed its ecclesiastical form. If anything, it becomes more ruthless. It is called the little horn. It is to be the power of religious authority over large political powers. This figure represents the entire period embracing Daniel's abomination of desolation.

The four-beast man of Daniel represents the four kingdoms that would dominate secular history until the appearance of that nation whose constitution and government would allow the establishment of that church whose scientific theology would eventually liberate all mankind from the slavery and tyranny of matter and sin. At this juncture, the Hebrew kingdom founded by David had been essentially destroyed by Babylon, but symbolically the government mentioned above would be a non-geographic restoration of David's kingdom on a scientific basis. The religion would eventually be recognized universally and would be known as Christian Science.

Babylon is represented by Daniel as gold, Media Persia as silver, Greece as bronze, and Rome as iron mixed with clay. Since gold is heavier than silver, silver heavier than bronze, and bronze heavier than iron mixed with clay, the figure is top-heavy. Of course the top-heavy figure must eventually fall. Rome lasted the longest, evolving from a secular to a tyrannical ecclesiastical state. The Science of the Christ born in the New Nation eventually would destroy the atheism and materialistic tyranny embodied in the figure, and all mankind would eventually be redeemed from the adamantine mesmerism that has appeared so real through the ages. Since Babylon is considered the cradle of civilization, it is natural that the head should represent Babylon. The secular intellect of all the nations was born there.

> "Four great beasts came up from the sea, diverse one from another" (Dan. 7:3).
> "These great beasts, which are four, are four kings, which shall arise out of the earth" (Dan. 7:17).

"The fourth beast shall be the fourth kingdom upon earth" (Dan. 7:23).

"After this I saw in the night visions, and behold a fourth beast, dreadful and terrible, and strong exceedingly; and it had great iron teeth: it devoured and brake in pieces, and stamped the residue with the feet of it: and it was diverse from all the beasts that were before it; and it had ten horns" (Dan. 7:7).

"I considered the horns, and behold, there came up among them another little horn, before whom there were three of the first horns plucked up by the roots: and, behold, in this horn were eyes like the eyes of man, and a mouth speaking great things" (Dan. 7:8).

There could hardly be a better description of the brute iron force of the Roman Empire. The Roman royal purple now floats like a poisonous vapor throughout Christendom, as Christendom is now redefined as the official religion of the state. In 533, Justinian's General Belisarius subdued the Vandal King Gelimer, restoring North Africa to the empire. In 540, Belisarius restored Ravenna to the empire, and finally in 552 Justinian's General Narses overthrew Totila, restoring Italy to the empire. Italy is again an integral part of the Roman Empire, an empire Justinian's two generals cleansed of non-Latin (Arian) theology. The first of Daniel's three horns to be overthrown was Italy under Odoacer—overthrown by the Gothic king Theodoric. The second horn, Italy under the Gothic king, was overthrown by the eastern emperor Justinian's General Belisarious and General Narses. There was exarchic rule of Italy now by the eastern emperor Justinian. The Lombards, under Alboin, eventually took most of Italy, including Rome. They were the third horn to rule Italy. Pepin and Charlemagne removed this third horn. They gave Rome to the pope. In the words of the Reverend John Cox, *On the Four Prophetic Empires and Kingdom of Messiah*, (Thames Ditton, Surrey: Leonard Seeley, 1845):

> The effects of this change were permanent and final. The last obstacle was now removed. The Pope rose at length to the temporal dominion, and

obtained a firm and settled place among the horns or kingdoms of the western empire. (P. 191)

In *The Church of the Sixth Century* (London: William Clowes & Sons, Ltd., 1897), W.H. Hutton writes:

Justinian, says the greatest English legal authority on his work, Mr. Bryce, probably never dreamt of the dangerous consequences which might follow the exemptions from civil jurisdiction which he conceded to the clergy, and the large powers of administering not only ecclesiastical but charitable property which he conferred upon the bishops ... to throw off the control of the civil power and even extend its own jurisdiction over civil causes." (P. 28)

Cox opined that "the 'Splendid Donation' was granted in supreme and absolute dominion; and the world beheld for the first time a Christian bishop invested with the prerogatives of a temporal prince." He continued:

From the time of the last emperor of the west these dynasties in succession appeared and wielded the scepter of nearly the whole of Italy, the Herule under Odoacer, Theodoric, and the Gothic Kings; and his Lombard Successors. Each of these, in succession, was overthrown in each case was effected by the direct aid and strenuous efforts of the Bishop of Rome, and ended in securing his dominion. This unknown and mysterious power was to arise amid the ten kingdoms of the west, soon after they appeared. It was to have a distinct seat and place in the body of the fourth empire and to exert a direct or indirect sovereignty over all the surrounding kings. These features can be found in no other power, whether past or future, but the Papacy at Rome. ... The spiritual claims of the

Papacy began just before its temporal dominions were acquired soon after the fall of the Western Empire. (*On the Four Prophetic Empires*, 192)

"After this I saw in the night visions, and behold a fourth beast, dreadful and terrible, and strong exceedingly; and it had great iron teeth: it devoured and brake in pieces, and stamped the residue with the feet of it: and it was diverse from all the beasts that were before it; and it had ten horns." Daniel 7:7

I considered the horns, and behold, there came up among them another little horn, before whom there were three of the first horns plucked up by the roots: and, behold, in this horn were eyes like the eyes of man, and a mouth speaking great things. Daniel 7:8

There could hardly be a better description of the brute iron force of the Roman Empire! The Roman royal purple now floats like a poisonous vapor throughout *Christendom* as Christendom is now redefined *the official religion* of the State. In 533 Justinian's General Belisarius subdued the Vandal King Gelimer, restoring North Africa to the Empire. In 540 Belisarius restored Ravenna to the Empire, and finally in 552 Justinian's General Narses overthrew Totila, restoring Italy to the empire, Italy is again an integral part of the Roman Empire, an empire Justinian's two generals *cleansed* of non Latin (Arian) theology. The first of Daniel's three horns to be overthrown was Italy under Odoacer—overthrown by the Gothic king Theodoric. The second horn, Italy under the Gothic king was overthrown by the eastern emperor Justinian's General Belisarious and General Narses. There was exarchic rule of Italy now by the eastern emperor Justinian. The Lombards, under Alboin, eventually took most of Italy, including Rome. They were the third hon to rule Italy. Pepin and Charlemagne removed this third horn They gave Rome to the Pope. In the words of John Cox:

The effects of this change were permanent and final. The last obstacle was now removed. The Pope rose at length to temporal dominion, and obtained a firm and settled place among the horns or kingdoms of the western empire.
On the Prophetic Empires and Kingdom of Messiah. Page 191

"Justinian, says the greatest English legal authority on his work, Mr. Bryce, 'probably never dreamt of the dangerous consequences which might follow the exemptions from civil jurisdiction which he conceded to the clergy, and the large powers of administering not only ecclesiastical but charitable property which he conferred upon the bishops. . . .to throw off the control of the civil power and even extend its own jurisdiction over civil causes."" (*Church of the Sixth Century*) W. H. Hutton

The Reverend John Cox opined "The 'Splendid Donation was granted in supreme and absolute dominion; and the world beheld for the first time a Christian bishop invested with the prerogatives of a temporal prince. . ."

From the time of the last emperor of the west these dynasties in succession appeared and wielded the scepter of nearly the whole of Italy, the Heruli under Odoacer, Theodoric, and the Gothic Kings; and his Lombard Successors. Each of these, in succession, was overthrown in each case was effected by the direct aid and strenuous efforts of the Bishop of

Little Horn Rome

Biblical Arithmology

Biblical arithmology is the term for the manner in which the Scriptural writers employed certain number combinations and usages. An understanding of such usage will make plain such Daniel expressions as *a time*, *times*, and *a portion of time*. The explanation will involve what is known as a Protestant reckoning.

The biblical prophets divined great significance in certain numbers and number combinations. However, there was absolutely nothing even resembling what is known as numerology. The *American College Dictionary* defines *numerology* as the "study of numbers ... supposedly to determine their influence on one's life and future." The biblical prophets suffered no illusions that numbers had some kind of inherent power of their own to influence or affect outcomes in any way. What were revealed to them were the times down into the future, and their use of numbers foresighted for them the times of future events.

The Hebrew lunar year was 360 days. The prophets called a lunar year *a time* and two lunar years (720 days) *times*. For one-half a lunar year (180 days), they used terms such as a *dividing* of time. However, they used what is known as the year-day system. What is meant by this? They used a lunar year (360 days) but substituted years for days. So 360 days were 360 years as they used it. From this, Daniel's *time*, *times* and *half-time* becomes 1,260 years (360 years + 720 years + 180 years). This same number of years is also found in the Apocalypse. The early Christians expected a rather immediate termination of "the times of the gentiles" and consequently a rather immediate Second Advent. They erred in not properly decoding the "days" used in the apocalyptic literature. There were also other reasons. Refer to Ezekiel 4:4-5:

> Lie thou also [on the ground] upon thy left side, and lay the iniquity of the house of Israel upon it: according to the number of the days that thou shalt lie upon it thou shalt bear iniquity.
>
> For I have laid upon thee the *years* [emphasis added] of their iniquity, according to the number of the *days*, [emphasis added], three hundred and ninety days: so shalt thou bear the iniquity of the house of Israel.

Here reference is made to the number of years the Davidic kingdom had drifted more and more into iniquity after the passing of David. Evidently there had been sufficient iniquity on the part of the people since David's time to warrant the Babylonian captivity as punishment. Thus begins the time of the gentiles. Numbers 14:34 refers to the forty days (years) the children of Israel spent in the Sinai wilderness with Moses:

> After the number of the days in which ye searched the land even forty days, each *day* [emphasis added] for a *year* [emphasis added], shall ye bear your iniquities, even forty years …

The following comments on the year/day system indicate its long usage:

> For a long time these principles have been so current among the expositors of the English and American world, that scarcely a serious attempt to vindicate them has of late been made. They have been regarded as *so plain* and so well *fortified* against *all objections* that most *expositors* have deemed it quite useless even to attempt to defend them. One might, indeed, almost compare the ready and unwavering assumption of these propo-

sitions to the assumption of the first self-evident axioms in the science of geometry, which not only may dispense with any process of ratiocination in their defense, but which do not even admit of any ...

And Professor Bush in writing to William Miller said:

In taking a *day* as the prophetical time for a *year,* I believe you are *sustained* by the soundest exegesis, as well as fortified by the high names of Mede, Sir Isaac Newton, Bishop Newton, Faber, Scott, Keith, and a host of others, who have long come to *substantially* your conclusions on this head. That all agree that the leading periods mentioned by Daniel and John [in Revelation] *do actually* expire about *this age of the world.*

In the twelfth chapter of Daniel in verse eleven, he adds an additional 30 days (years), and in verse twelve yet an additional 45 days (years). Daniel's numerical quantities were, therefore, 1,260 years; 1,290 years (1260 years + 30 years); and 1,335 years (1,290 years + 45 years). These three periods of years are the Daniel prophetic periods addressed in this work.

In his prophecies for what he foresaw, Daniel's prophetic structure is mathematically unique. He foresees the ultimate triumph of the ancient truth which the Hebrews of his time had been unable to maintain, or for that matter, sufficiently understand in order to maintain.

His structure is built around several periods of time lasting one or more of the time constants listed above. Each period he refers to as an abomination of desolation. He even talks about the "daily sacrifice" being taken away during the period of the abominations. That sacrifice was central to the nature of Hebrew worship, and its loss would be of stupendous importance. Moses had written the entire book of Leviticus developing its involved procedure.

These abominations would represent periods in which authoritarian power would grossly invade the rights of conscience, especially religious and medical conscience. The *abomination* and *desolation* terms show just how overwhelmingly evil these periods were to be. Since the desolations were to last a given period of time, what must it be like at the termination of a given desolation time? The writer sought to answer not only that question but also to uncover the beginning of such periods.

This set the writer in search of significant periods in history that might fit. His choice of events was not hasty but chosen carefully in accord with what, to him, seemed appropriate. To his satisfaction, the end of each desolation period culminated in a societal, political, or religious event or events that tended to reverse the evil of the preceding period. The final desolation period ended, in the writer's view, with the coming of the Second Advent.

Thus the ancient Hebrew truth, and especially the Messianic outcome therefrom, was restored by the Second Advent when the woman with the leaven, as prophesied by our beloved Master, brought the science of that which lay behind his incredible life to mankind.

Daniel's prophetic times, including the important dates corresponding thereto, are completely developed by a series of graphic time arrows covering the abomination periods. They tell the whole story as the author sees it. An accompanying text, however, has been written for the reader whose interest may cause him to prefer a fuller and more detailed elaboration of the information carried in the time arrows. The time arrows are necessary to illustrate the time periods, and the text should be read in conjunction with them.

Each of the writer's choice of historical commencing dates of Daniel's four abomination periods is a date clearly initiating one of the four pivotal historical events causing the emergence of political Rome into ecclesiastical, or little horn, Rome. Events commencing from any one of the four periods and following one of Daniel's time periods (1,260 years, 1,290 years, 1,335 years) therefrom are concatenated historical events sequentially causing the ultimate dissolution of the little horn power and the enabling of political, social, and legal conditions necessary for the emergence of the Second Advent.

The above paragraph is a summation of the significance of Daniel's biblical arithmology. The pages that follow are the detailed fleshing-out.

Modern scholars generally have concluded, based largely on language and "internal evidence" in the Book of Daniel, that Daniel's visions included gentile world rule extending from the Babylonians through the Greeks but not including the Romans. This limited view was not held by most of the senior period scholars, however, and Dr. Cyrus Ingerson Schofield does not endorse it. This view is not universally held even by modern scholars, and in the author's view, such a concept would truncate the prophet's incredible insights into the ultimate "end times" of the nations, limiting them to an interim end time. To the author there is a certain artificiality in their view, which may be understandable since the remarkable synchronisms of Daniel's dates with respect to modern times is either rejected or not perceived by them. In any case, scholars even disagree on the force of the arguments of language and internal evidence against Daniel's visions extending beyond the Greek period. Actually, the modern view is really not modern so much as a rebirth of the neo-Platonic teaching of the infidel Porphyry.

The Scriptural Hebrews always regarded history and treated with it only insofar as it affected the Hebrew people. This view at first glance might appear parochial and naive, but further reflection should temper such a conclusion. They clearly saw that the God of Israel represented the only significant fact with which mankind ultimately had to deal and that the ancient Hebrews had a singular proclivity to perceive His nature and significance. Thus they, through their spiritual leaders, comprised the custodial trust who would keep the torch burning until the God of Israel should be adored by all the races on earth as the reign of materialism waned.

Abomination is from the Latin *ab omen* (a thing of ill omen), and according to the *Standard Dictionary,* originally applied to anything held in religious or ceremonial aversion or abhorrence. Apparently this particular thing of religious abhorrence was going to desolate and scatter the power of the holy people. *Desolate* is from the Latin *de* (entirely) + *solus* (alone). So apparently this thing of ill omen was destined to have some kind of power to destroy the collective and cohesive strength of God's people, effectively isolating them into a terrible spiritual aloneness leaving any with a remaining scintilla of spiritual light entirely alone and isolated. This was evidently going to happen to the followers of the Messiah in the First Advent for the *time of the end*, when all of this would begin to pass, is synonymous with the Second Advent. Just how all of these things were to take place will be dealt with in the chapters following.

Again, the daily sacrifice literally involved the sacrifice of animals at the temple in Jerusalem. But this practice only symbolized a deeper significance and indeed the only significance vital to the ultimate redemption of mankind from the atheism of flesh beliefs. The sacrifice of animal flesh obviously couldn't liberate mankind from these flesh beliefs, but the symbolism of that practice at least foreshadowed the ultimate sacrifice of the belief that we are imprisoned in flesh with no route of escape. Moses' complex ritual of how to handle the different parts of the ritual animal's body hints of this. When the Jews were forbidden to perform the daily sacrifice, this did but foreshadow a later forbidding performing the daily sacrifice on a higher level than animal sacrifice. This taking away of the daily sacrifice in the higher sense commenced simultaneously with the abomination. What was this higher sense? Remember Jesus' response to the disciples' question concerning their inability to heal the epileptic? He told them that prayer and fasting were required. It is no secret that sacrifice of daily food won't heal epilepsy. Isn't it obvious then that Jesus referred to a sacrifice of the false food of belief in material medical laws of the flesh governing man? This kind of daily sacrifice was ultimately to be proscribed by a state-enforced religion whose theology actually forbad spiritual healing. And this proscription was to be essentially simultaneous with the early church's establishment of hospitals.

The woman fleeing into the wilderness is symbolically the last event to take place in the virtual total disappearance of primitive Christianity. Spirituality seems in general to appear more easily to feminine than to masculine thinking. Thus the woman in the wilderness became the archetype in the Scriptures for the spirituality of the church. In this connection, it must be remembered that the Edenic Covenant to Eve was that she (a woman) was to bruise the head of the serpent (or destroy evil). This covenant was positively *not* given to Adam (the masculine thought). It is most natural that the Messiah should come through the purest of feminine thought, the issue of a virgin. Clearly Adam, the masculine thought, had to be totally unconnected with the Master's nativity, and only through a virgin birth was this possible. The covenant given to Eve ultimately required the virgin birth as a condition of fulfillment. Mary of Nazareth (fulfilling the Genesis promise to another Eve) had the spirituality to receive the angel message from the eternal Father, which enabled her to give our Master a birth free of lust and passion or carnal desire. He must have this head start in purity in order to properly acquit his mission so indispensible to mortals' salvation from the fatal triad of masculine conviction (sin, sickness, and death). It is encouraging to see evidence of a growing feminine influence in the Latin church. The statement by the late pope that *Mother* more nearly represented God than Father was a beacon of light!

The Number 666

The Apocalypse gives the coded number 666 and says it is the number of a man's name. It further shows that the name is the key as to who will be in power during the time of the great tribulation, the period of the abomination of desolation. Now since both the Apocalypse and Daniel prophesy the era of a time, times, and a dividing of time, the periods of the great tribulation, this coded number should be decoded. Irenaeus was a pupil of Polycarp, who was a student of the beloved disciple John, who wrote the Apocalypse after Jesus' ascension; nevertheless, the message was given to him from Jesus according to John himself. Irenaeus says that the number applies to "Latinos" (Henry H. Halley, *Halley's Bible Handbook,* [Grand Rapids: Zondervan Publishing House], 726). This is the Greek for the king who gave name to the Latin empire. In the old languages, number-values were assigned to the letters of their respective alphabets. In the Greek alphabet, L is equal to thirty, A is equal to one, T is equal to three hundred, E is equal to five, I is equal to ten, N is equal to fifty, O is equal to seventy, and S is equal to two hundred. These numbers sum to six hundred and sixty-six and correspond to a man's name, Latinos (see Rev. 13:18). Since Daniel has identified the Roman Empire already in the man's image with the legs of iron and feet of clay mixed with iron, and also as the beast with the iron teeth and the stomping feet, it is useful to have a second identification by someone like Irenaeus identifying, to his satisfaction, what Jesus apparently revealed to John: namely, the 666 code. From the symbolic code, unmistakably we are dealing with a form of the Roman Empire, especially in its later, ecclesiastical, little horn incarnation. Irenaeus was close to the beloved John's student Polycarp, who was one of the great martyrs for Christianity.

Preface

Should there be any justification required for developing a work of this kind, the author will defer to the judgment of Sir Isaac Newton, of whom, concerning his mental capacities, even the great Albert Einstein said, "We stand on his shoulders." Einstein had great respect for Newton's work on Daniel's prophecies, had them in his library, and he certainly considered him a giant in the global history of original thinking. Newton writes:

> As the few and obscure prophecies concerning Christ's first coming were for setting up the Christian religion, which all nations have corrupted; so, the many and clear prophecies concerning the things to be done at His second coming are not only for predicting but also for effecting, a recovery and establishment of the long-lost truth, and setting up a kingdom wherein dwelleth righteousness. (*The Time of the End*, 314)

Any attempt to unlock Daniel's prophesies for the "last-days" is daunting, but this does not mean it cannot be done. The writer has satisfied himself that his efforts have borne fruit. His efforts parallel some of the results of the earliest century's expositors. Most of their efforts are covered in the book, *The Time of the End*. There is one very great difference between the writer's analysis and theirs. Although the writer initially was convinced, as they were, that the beginning of Daniel's abomination of desolation had a single beginning and a single ending (the final one), he was ultimately compelled to the conclusion that there were four beginnings and four endings, i.e., four abomination-of-desolation periods leading to the final historical emancipation.

According to the first volume of the *Anchor Bible Dictionary,* most modern scholars hold that a more accurate translation of the *abomination of desolation* phrase from Daniel is *appalling sacrilege.* These scholars argue that Daniel might have meant both, for what came was indeed abominable, and it desolated the true church. The early expositors of Daniel's abominations concluded that there was only one such period. They had to choose what they considered the primary or most significant historical event beginning a true historical abomination leading in 1,260 years to a glorious liberation and Second Advent sort of condition. They, nonetheless, puzzled over earlier periods following which there was much darkness. This caused them to choose different historical events to start their abomination calculations from. This led to different final end-time conclusions.

The periods of the appalling sacrilege were freighted with significance. They hosted the 325 A.D. Nicaean Council, which essentially ended true Christianity as Jesus practiced it and set the stage for Daniel's abominations of desolation. It opened the door for developing enormous power of the clergy over the people and introduced, through the Trinity theory, polytheism into Christianity.

As we shall see, the transmutation of the political western half of the Roman Empire into its ecclesiastical form (Dan. 7:8), i.e., the rise of Daniel's little horn, was the final total paganization of the Christianity of the First Advent. The Bishop of Rome (little horn) had manipulated and brought about all three of these overthrowings and finally was given a large portion of Italy, including ten cities and the city of Rome, by Pepin and Charlemagne, the last ones to overthrow. As a temporal power, the little horn did not possess the vastness of territory the other ten horns had, and thusly Daniel's little horn. But as a power over the minds and bodies of men, the little horn made the others pale in significance.

The ten toes represent the ten horns in their "mingling" aspects, and hence the "iron mixed with clay." Pure iron, figuratively, does not break apart!

The little horn is mental, not physical. It has eyes like a man yet retains a mouth of iron teeth. Could this be symbolic of the devouring of the people's true sense of spirituality, their spiritual substance, even as the ancient political or state empire had devoured the people's material substance if they didn't please the emperor?

Ecclesiastical Rome, or Rome of the little horn, took an iron grip on the minds of men, threatening eternal damnation, and if that didn't work, influenced the civil government to prosecute and punish what they called heretics. These, of course, were individuals or organizations such as the Waldensians, or later the Hugenots, who didn't accept the official theology. It even included some of their very own, such as the redoubtable Girolamo Savonarola.

Daniel refers to the eyes of the little horn as being stouter than his fellows. One definition of *see* is Episcopal in nature and designates the authority or power of a bishop. Was there a double entendre here?

But first there had to be some definite cleavage between the Eastern or Byzantine Empire and the Western Empire, for Daniel's prophecy deals virtually exclusively with the West. Cox's description of the cleavage is excellent:

> This unknown and mysterious power was to arise amid the ten kingdoms of the west, soon after they appeared. It was to have a distinct seat and place in the body of the fourth empire [Rome]. At the same time it was to claim a prophetic character, and to exert a direct or indirect sovereignty over all the surrounding kings. These features can be found in no other power, whether past or future, but the Papacy at Rome. ... The spiritual claims of the Papacy began just before its temporal dominions were acquired soon after the fall of the Western Empire. (*On The Four Prophetic Empires,* 152)

The writer concluded that all of the earlier events were part of the principle or 606 A.D. event, when *de jure* power was bestowed upon the little horn, and that an abomination period counted from each of them would lead toward the result of the final event.

Figure 2 deals with the period when the ten-horn political empire was changing into the little horn, or ecclesiastical, empire, still ten-horned but the ten horns essentially under control of a single *virtual* horn—the little horn. Cox generates a table of the varying ten kingdoms from the beginning (after Valens and beginning with Augustulus). The number hovers about the number ten all the way to the year 1816 and is frequently, but not always, exactly ten. His explanation:

> Amidst fluctuations so numerous and unceasing as almost to defy an exact numeration. The prophetic description [of Daniel] remains prominent and a tenfold division of the Western Empire reappears from time to time. The correspondence with the prediction [of Daniel] is thus accurate and complete. For it must be borne in mind that two opposite features had really to be fulfilled. The tenfold number was to exist; but there was also to be a frequent intermingling with the seed of men. In the actual outline of European history, both of these predicted features are alike conspicuous. (*On the Four Prophetic Empires*, 152)

Of course, as Cox has noted elsewhere, Daniel never implied that the ten kingdoms would be the same throughout the Roman beast's history but simply that there would always be a ten-kingdom division. Cox refers to the difficulty of pinpointing an exact ten due to the fluctuations brought about by Daniel's equally valid *intermingling* prophecy. The writer, however, was not too satisfied with the two prophecies possibly conflicting.

In the table referred to above, Cox lists two sets of numbers representing the number of kingdoms existing simultaneously over approximately half-century intervals. One set of numbers represents kingdoms, or horns, of unquestionable autonomy. The other set lists these kingdoms as well as additional kingdoms that may be under the real control of one of the other kingdoms, and thus not fully qualify as an independent horn. Secular history is not quite clear on this. All of this, again, was brought about by the mingling-caused fluctuations. The author took the statistical average of both sets of numbers and then took the statistical average of these two averages. The pleasant result was the number ten! This more precisely justifies Daniel's prophecy that there would be ten horns throughout the beast's history.

The first chapter dealing with the four abominations begins with the Nicene Council of 325 A.D. This is the year when the mighty Roman Empire mandated Christianity as the official Roman religion, and from this followed all the horrors of the Dark Ages, including the Inquisition. This is the year when tritheism was introduced into Christianity.

Most of the early expositors chose the year 606 as their significant commencement. This was the year *de jure* power was bestowed upon the Roman bishop, and consequently the year of the absolute, unequivocal little-horn church and state union leading to the Dark Ages. Each beginning initiated a condition that further enslaved mankind's mind and freedom. Each ending was the beginning of a loosening or breaking of the chain link enslaving mankind, and a necessary prelude to the next beginning. The final beginning and ending represented the breaking of the last link of the chain binding mankind. Little could Newton have envisioned the nature and form his insight would take! The Second Advent has arrived, and is shaking the nations. This shaking is not at the present time perceived by mankind in general.

The writer unequivocally considers that Mary Baker Eddy's discovery of Christian Science in 1866 ushered in the Second Advent and accepts without doubt these words of hers in connection with her church: "... the divine Spirit, imperatively propelling the greatest moral, physical, civil, and religious reform ever known on earth" (*Pulpit and Press,* [Boston: The First Church of Christ, Scientist], 20). The author accepts that Mary of Bow, New Hampshire, ushered in the "spirit of truth" that our dear Master prophesied even as Mary of Nazareth ushered in the First Advent with the virgin birth. The first Mary's child, "the only begotten," proved the absolute power of God over biological process. The second Mary's child was a discovery that unfolded the science that lay behind the work of the first Mary's child. It should appear most natural to the Bible scholar that the two Advents should be the outcome of the feminine thought, directed by the Creator, for in Genesis 3:4 we read: "And I will put enmity between thee and the woman, and between thy seed and her seed; it shall bruise thy head, and thou shalt bruise [bite] his heel." Here God was talking to the serpent, the symbol of all evil, the evil that was to be destroyed by the two Advents. This verse seems almost certainly a prophecy of the two Advents! Notice that the enmity was between woman's seed and the serpent, not between man's seed and the serpent. This explains further why Jesus had to be virgin-conceived! Eddy was the human fulfillment of Jesus' "woman with the leaven." Dear reader, we are the early benefactors of this "magnificent manifestation"—God's second Witness, long foretold by the ancient prophets, standing with her Galilean brother to effect a metamorphosis destined to utterly destroy the atheism of matter. The man image of Daniel (Figure 1) is the beginning symbol of what will be discussed in this work. This symbol represented the four kingdoms that were to rule the world in the period referred to by the prophets as the "times of the gentiles." The rule of the gentiles commenced after the Babylonian captivity (circa 607 B.C.), as this was the end of the Davidic kingdom—the only theocracy coming directly from the Mosaic Law and the prophets, excepting the era of the Judges. It was lost because of disobedience to that upon which it was founded and based. Daniel was one of the captives, but he was so well thought of by the king as to be made prime minister of Babylon. Daniel actually prophesied the rise of the four main gentile kingdoms preceding the Second Advent. The higher criticism biblical scholars, coming largely out of Germany during the nineteenth century, cite what they call internal problems with the book of Daniel itself, such as language changes, differing styles, and so forth, to denominate Daniel at best an historian or at least largely fictional as a prophet. Porphyry, the Neo-Platonist known for his violent hatred of Christianity and promotion of paganism, wrote scathingly during the third century about Daniel and denominated him at best an historian. One wonders if the Germans didn't take a note out of his book. I could continue on with a litany of modern higher critics and their tedious dismantling of that which makes Daniel what he really is, but won't honor the scholastic tedium. There is one major problem with all of them. Jesus of Nazareth considered Daniel a prophet, not an historian, and so referred to him!

Daniel traces several lines or directions of prophecy in his book. The author has pursued two of them, and this work concerns one of these, essentially chapters seven and twelve. The present work concerns itself primarily with the prophetic content of the man image, characterized by Daniel as a beast, which is treated in detail in the Daniel chapters seven and twelve. Nebuchadnezzar, the Babylonian king, dreamed about the four-tiered image. Daniel interpreted the dream for the king. He said:

> Thou, O king, sawest, and behold a great image. This great image, whose brightness was excellent, stood before thee; This image's head was of fine gold, his breast and his arms of silver, his belly and his thighs of brass, His legs of iron, his feet part of iron and part of clay. Thou sawest till that a stone was cut out without hands, which smote the image upon his feet that were of iron and clay, and brake them to pieces. Then was the iron, the clay, the brass, the silver, and the gold, broken to pieces together, and became like the chaff of the summer threshing floors; and the wind carried them away, that no place was found for them: and the stone that smote the image became a great mountain, and filled the whole earth. (Dan. 2:31-35)

Figure 1 is a graphical representation of this image as Daniel describes him.

Chapter eight deals with Antiochus Epiphanies also characterized as a beast, but he so adumbrated Daniel's final little horn, the little horn of chapter seven, as to be an actual prototype foreshadowing the coming of the final little horn. A graphical representation of the City Foursquare would embrace the spherical symbols of an existence which has no beginning and no ending and "all sense of error disappears and thought accepts the divine infinite calculus" (Mary Baker Eddy, *Science and Health with Key to the Scriptures,* [The First Church of Christ, Scientist], 520). Daniel knew that a transcendent state awaited mankind following what he denominated "the end time." He, of course, could hardly have envisioned its ultimate grandeur in that era even as it is difficult for us who are living in the early part of the final prophetic era. Eddy also wrote: "Mind is perpetual motion. Its symbol is the sphere" (*Science and Health,* 240) and "Advancing spiritual steps in the teeming universe of Mind lead on to spiritual spheres and exalted beings" (ibid., 513).

This final arrival of Daniel's end time of the rule of the gentiles, of course, will happen simultaneously when the impact of the stone in the man image of Figure 1 fully strikes the legs of that image. This is true because in a broader sense, the image really represents the totality of all governmental, civil, social, clerical, medical, or legal interference with the rights of conscience or anything that would run counter to the sentiments of the First Amendment of the Constitution of the United States, a sacred document clothed in secular garments.

Benjamin Rush, signer of the Declaration of Independence and personal physician to George Washington, had this to say: "I do not believe that the Constitution was the offspring of inspiration but I am perfectly satisfied the union of the States in its form and adoption is as much the work of a Divine Providence as any of the miracles recorded in the Old and New Testaments." Rush also wrote: "Unless we put medical freedom into the Constitution, the time will come when medicine will organize into an undercover dictatorship. To restrict the art of healing to one class of men and deny equal privileges to others will constitute the Bastille of medical science. All such laws are un-American and despotic and have no place in a republic. The Constitution of this republic should make special privilege for medical freedom as well as religious freedom" (*Letters of Benjamin Rush,* vol. 1, [Princeton, NJ: American Philosophical Society, 1951], 475).

It even protects—at the present time—forces which are anything but godlike, but in the fullness of time this will change! Daniel's abomination periods preceded the coming of the Second Advent, but these other forms keep persisting worldwide in various guises. Ultimately of course, each of us, by the choices we make, is individually responsible for his or her own salvation, and individual atonement must be attained. Still, it is interesting to ponder the following words of Eddy in *The People's Idea of God* (Boston: The First Church of Christ, Scientist):

> The legislators who are greatly responsible for *all* [emphasis added] the woes of mankind are those leaders of public thought who are mistaken in their methods of humanity. (P. 11)

And Eddy in *Science and Health*:

> The law of the divine Mind must end human bondage, or mortals will continue unaware of man's inalienable rights and in subjection to hopeless slavery, because *Some public teachers* [emphasis added] permit an ignorance of divine power,—an ignorance that is the foundation of continued bondage and of human suffering. (P. 227)

And finally, Eddy writes in *The People's Idea of God:*

> The lame, the blind, the sick, the sensual, are slaves, and their fetters are gnawing away life and hope: their chains are clasped by the false teachings, false theories, false fears that enforce new forms of oppression, and are the modern Pharaohs that hold the children of Israel still in bondage. (P. 11)

And so Eddy evaluates the effect of the modern Pharaohs on individual salvation! These are the modern pagan teachings and are still represented by the man image, the essence of human will.

Do the ancient roots of paganism change at all simply because its modern leaders wear an Oxford suit or perhaps clerical robes or are clothed in the hospital garments of Aesculapius? The largest percentage of this human mischief is probably promulgated by a mistaken sense of right, but that doesn't lessen its devastating effect.

While we are individually responsible for the conduct leading to our own entering into the kingdom, there is an unmistakable indication in the above three quotes that the rock of Christian Science must literally smash into oblivion the feet of the top-heavy beast! In other words, there is an implied institutional responsibility for some of the difficulties in working out individual salvation. The Daniel period of prophecy was a period characterized as the periods of the *great tribulation*.

Some have believed that at the Second Advent tribulation will cease. This will come to pass, however, only when the world recognizes its reappearance has already occurred. Jesus promised that which should come would lead into all truth, would be the absolute science of his teaching, but he figuratively added: "When the Son of man cometh will he find faith on the earth?" In other words, will the Second Advent be recognized at first? Christian Science will ultimately be accepted as the phenomenon of the Second Advent. Tribulation will ultimately melt into the abyss.

This text is structured around six illustrated arrows. Arrows 4-7 represent Daniel's biblical arithmology embracing a time, times, and half of a time. It forms a concatenated series of times, each roughly corresponding to a time, times, and a half of a time.

This work contains an arrow text describing the significance of each arrow.

As discussed above, the writer began with the impression that there was only one time period representing Daniel's time, times, and one-half a time, and consequently only one arrow. As it happens, he began to realize that there were several end-to-end arrows. The preceding arrow themes became reinforcements for each new arrow. The structure became similar to that of a Beethoven symphony. First a theme is heard rather softly, and then it is repeated, with theme variation of some sort more loudly until the full thrust of the theme is apparent.

Daniel's abomination of desolation, or time of great tribulation, always begins with an event that chains mankind's moral freedom followed by an event (generally a time, times, and a half time—1,260 years later) that tends to nullify or weaken for mankind the original binding event or condition. This is the line of experience leading to the Second Advent.

Finally, this work is the writer's sole opinion and interpretation of Scripture and prophecy. So far as he knows, neither individual nor organization, religious or otherwise, holds similar views or ideas, although some of the old divines of several centuries ago had similar views and insight. The writer assumes full responsibility for the ideas put forth in this work. He has been quite grateful for the help of Patricia Billingsley, a very dear friend of many years, for editorial and literary help and advice.

Finally, each arrow page contains sufficient written information to allow a comprehension of the significant beginning and end of a Daniel period. The text that follows is simply a more fully developed text on the events and should allow a deeper comprehension of the significance of the relevant events.

The Fall of the Empire

The year 453 A.D. was essentially the beginning of the fall of the Western Roman Empire as a political state. The following chapters deal with its metamorphoses into an ecclesiastical entity. The terrible ten-horned beast with great iron teeth and stomping feet (Dan. 7:7) had been severely wounded by a number of things: the incursion of Germanic tribes breaking up its monolithic culture and sacking Rome, and the fact that the empire had been split into two branches, the eastern, or Byzantine, branch being headquartered in Constantinople, and the western in Rome. And there were many other causes. It might be worthwhile here to quote Edward Gibbon from his *Decline and Fall of the Roman Empire:*

> As early as the time of Cicero and Varro it was the opinion of the Roman augurs that the twelve vultures which Romulus had seen represented the twelve centuries assigned for the fatal period of his city. This prophecy, disregarded perhaps in the season of health and prosperity, inspired the people with gloomy apprehensions when the twelfth century, clouded with disgrace and misfortune, was almost elapsed; and even posterity must acknowledge with some surprise that the arbitrary interpretation of an accidental or fabulous circumstance has been seriously verified in the downfall of the Western empire. But its fall was announced by a clearer omen than that of the flight of vultures: The

Roman government appeared every day less formidable to its enemies, more obvious and oppressive to its subjects. The taxes were multiplied with the public distress; economy was neglected in proportion as it became necessary; and the injustice of the rich shifted the unequal burden from themselves to the people. (P. 102)

Here Gibbon is pinpointing the ultimate decline and fall of even the ecclesiastical or little horn empire. It is evident here from Gibbon that an ecclesiastical state really cares very little for the people. So much for a false sense of deific worship.

It is difficult to choose the worst condition, whether it is the excessive theological cruelty of the earlier little horn Roman bishops or the corrupt and immoral behavior of an Alexander Borgia. The moral rectitude of the earlier ones did in no way modify their disregard for the Sixth Commandment in the name of religious authority. In short, the mixing of church and state is good for no one!

The importance of all this to our Daniel prophecies is this: The *sorely wounded beast* was to recover under the form of Daniel's little horn, i.e., ecclesiastical Rome, although there was a temporary political resurgence under the Byzantine emperor Justinian who, ironically, through his subject Tribonian's brilliant legal mind, distilled the Roman law in such a manner as to set the stage for the staggering secular power of the Bishop of Rome.

From Martin Luther to Mary Baker Eddy

Revelation 19:6 says, "There shall be time no longer." From the Greek, "time" as used here refers not to time such as a clock ticking, but refers to a *period* of time such as a week or a day or a month. If the period referred to is a prophetic time, it refers to the Hebrew prophetic year. And so the text should be properly translated: Three hundred and sixty years, or "a time," shall not pass before the prophecy is fulfilled. The prophecy was "… the mystery of God should be finished" (Rev. 10:7). Luther's Reformation was the nuclear blast that broke the hold of the little horn and started Bible reading again for other than just the clergy. This was a necessary preclusion to the introduction of the Science destined to remove the "mystery of God" from the Scriptures. Three hundred and fifty-eight years (the time from the Reformation to the publication of Eddy's *Science and Health*) falls just short of a prophetic year, a direct fulfillment of Revelation 10:6. Luther's ordination was in the year 1507. This ordination represented the beginning of Luther's career and created the opportunity for the Reformation. This date also was just short of one prophetic year from the beginning of the year of the Second Advent—the discovery of Christian Science! Luther lived toward the close (76 percent) of the time interval of the sixth seal of Revelation. Eddy writes in *Science and Health* that as early as 1862, she began to "write down and give to friends, the results of her Scriptural study." And Revelation 10:7 says that "in the days of the voice of the Seventh angel … the mystery of God should be finished." When the science concerning something is discovered, the subject is no longer a mystery. Fenes Clinton, a nineteenth-century Bible scholar considered an expert on Scriptural chronology, wrote in his *Essay on Scriptural Chronology* that the year 1862 would appear exactly six thousand years since Adam. This would designate that history from 1862 onward would be the story of the Seventh Millennium. (Christian Science is the significant event of the Seventh millennium).

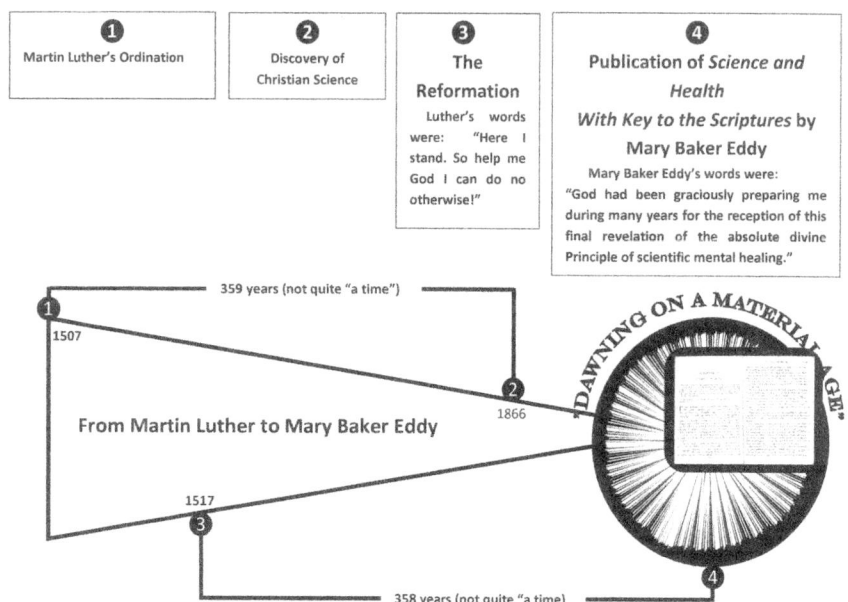

Chapter I
Luther and the Reformation

The Wagnerian thunder of Luther's Teutonic Reformation released a nucleonic force that had first to reverberate throughout England's hills and vales and across her poetic lochs in order to set the conditions for the Plymouth Rock experience. Even England was not up to the impending revolution of freeing the religious conscience. Cranmer and others would vouch for that! However, it was the Protestant discipline that fitted the English mind to thwart the designs of the beast and thus begin the fulfillment of the latter-day elements of Daniel's prophecy. It was this Protestant imperative that prepared the thought of the Second witness from childhood. It was the Protestant discipline sailing out of England that prepared our founding fathers to compose the immortal documents that were destined to give legal protection to the child of the "woman in travail." Luther broke the thrall that had held Europe in magnetic hypnotism since the fall of secular Rome and the beginning of the machinations of the little horn. It was no casual allusion enshrining Plymouth as the New Canaan. New England was destined to be the birth of the Second Advent! The voyage began with a ship sailing from Plymouth, England, which brought Luther's thunder to the Plymouth of the new world. It will end with the total salvation of mankind's release from the adamantine superstition that matter is anything but an illusion!

In *Beacon Lights of History* (New York: James Clarke and Co., 1902), John Lord wrote, "Luther moved Europe by ideas that emancipated the millions and set in motion a progress which is the glory of our age" (305). Luther inaugurated a mass death of false gods. His massive, historic *der Gotterdammerung* was indeed the twilight of the gods, the relatively short time left before the scientific beginning of the destruction of the false gods of coercive fear, ecclesiastical tyranny, and imperialistic power over man's life and consciousness, but most importantly, a gradual freeing from the enslavement of Aesculapian priesthood theories of medicine resulting in a return to Jesus' teaching of healing the sick through the divine Spirit. In short, the forged chain lengths imprisoning man's medical, political, personal, and religious freedom were to be broken. These links were already developing, but the forging and ultimate hardening occurred when *de jure* power, beginning with the emperor Phocas, concerning religion, was granted to religious priesthood by the Roman emperor. Phocas was under the influence of Frederic for years. Christian healing, as Jesus taught it, was waning and vanished about the time of the Nicene Council.

Benjamin Rush's prediction has become fact. The hosts of Aesculapius rule the medical world today, a system of medicine coming originally out of pagan Greece, legally, even in the United States, replacing the healing practice taught by our Master. Rush's phrase "undercover dictatorship" was uncannily precise. The legal force from the judicial bench forcing *materia medica* upon the unwilling individual is legendary and even greatly praised by some who think they know best what is good for others!

Daniel's 1,260-year intervals were required to break each link in this chain of religious tyranny, including the final one where the *de jure* power was granted. The chain had to be destroyed sufficiently to open the way for the appearing of the Second Advent.

With the Second Advent came the key to that compilation which Luther had made available to the common man: the Holy Scriptures. This key was destined eventually to unlock the gates of heaven for all mankind. First the book had to be given back to the people. Luther did that. Second, the depths of its meaning had to be unlocked. The Messenger of the Second Advent did that; and in her pamphlet "No and Yes" (Boston: The First Church of Christ, Scientist), Mary Baker Eddy writes that "no

Reign of Terror or rule of error will again unite Church and State, or reenact, through the civil arm of government, the horrors of religious persecution" (44). She also writes: "As descendants of Puritans, let us lift their standard higher, rejoicing, as Paul did, that we are *free born."* Additionally, Eddy writes: "I love the prosperity of Zion, be it promoted by Catholic, by Protestant, or by Christian Science, which anoints with Truth, opening the eyes of the blind and healing the sick" (*The First Church of Christ, Scientist and Miscellany,* [Boston: The First Church of Christ, Scientist], 270). She alludes several times in her vast writings to the medical doctors eventually practicing strictly Christian Science healing as Jesus did it!

The following chapter will discuss and explicate the meaning and use of prophetic numbers as used in the Scriptures.

Finally, these words Elaine Pagels writes in *Adam, Eve, and the Serpent* (New York: Random House) are relevant: "Yet, as we have seen, Christians during the first centuries would not have imagined that their vision of a society characterized by liberty and justice could be the basis for a political agenda. ... Centuries, even millennia, would pass before such visions began to inform actual political aspirations and institutions; and only the most optimistic among us may still hope that such visions will one day achieve political reality" (149).

Such vision will come about only when the acceptance of Christian Science becomes more widespread. But it certainly will not happen under Augustine theology. But there is a step beyond Pagels's vision. Following the realization of her vision is the total redemption of mankind from the "atheism of matter." Eddy, the messenger of the Second Advent, writes in *Science and Health* (233) that "in the midst of imperfection, perfection is seen and acknowledged only by degrees. The ages must slowly work up to perfection. How long it must be before we arrive at the demonstration of scientific being, no man knoweth,—not even 'the Son but the Father;' but the false claim of error continues until the goal of goodness is assiduously earned and won."

First Abomination Period

❶
Constantine and the Nicene Council

The emperor Constantine declares Christianity the official religion of the Roman Empire with its inevitable paganization leading to the Dark Ages. In defiance of the First Commandment, it was here that tritheism (the polytheism of three gods) was introduced into Christianity, the religion of the First Advent, causing Christian healing to be displaced by *materia medica* hospitals, i.e. after Jesus came to be regarded as one of three gods in the Godhead the healing power he practiced on earth could not have been done by a mere man, but by a god. Since men are not gods, what was left of Christian healing was inevitably finally lost following this ecumenical event whose decisions became the basis of "Christian" theology for centuries. It is not surprising; following the **pagan** nation's adoption of Christianity, that Jesus' Christian method of healing by the power of God was replaced by the Aesculapian medicine of **pagan** Greece. But, then, Rome always borrowed her pagan culture from Greece. This council set the stage for the rule of Daniel's *little horn* (the evolutionary metamorphosis of Rome from a powerful pagan political empire into a powerful, intolerant and inquisitorial ecclesiastical empire). Horn is used in Scripture to indicate a ruling power, and staggering power the little horn, though little, was gradually to develop. Perhaps the most egregious effect on mankind's future happiness and freedom was the adoption of Greek *materia medica*. This practice carried over even into the American Republic. Dr. Benjamin Rush, signer of the Declaration of Independence and personal physician to George Washington said, "Unless we put medical freedom into the Constitution, the time will come when medicine will organize into an undercover dictatorship. . .To restrict the art of healing to one class of men [the hosts of Aesculapius] and deny equal privileges to others will constitute the Bastille of medical science. All such laws are un-American and despotic and have no place in a republic. . . The Constitution of the republic should make special privilege for medical freedom as well as religious freedom.

Phillip Schaft writes in *History of the Christian Church*. "The Athanasius Creed closes the succession of ecumenical symbols, symbols which are acknowledged by the entire orthodox Christian world, except that Evangelical Protestantism ascribes to them not an absolute but only a relative authority, and reserves the right of freely investigating and further developing all church doctrines from the inexhaustible fountain of the infallible word of God.' God speed this development!

❷
The great Armada
Open war with Britain begun, terminating with British defeat of the Spanish.

This had the effect of making irreversible the reestablishment by Elizabeth I, as far as she would let it, of Luther's Protestant Reformation's arrival in England.

Although Luther's theology did not challenge the fundamental Nicene error of tritheism it did effectively remove Christianity from central bureaucratic (*little horn*) control so that it could be eventually cleansed of this gross violation of the First Commandment. Luther's thunderous reformation was the first significant step in this important cleansing. But it first had to be delivered to the New World. The Mayflower did that!

❸
Plymouth
Captain John Smith of the Virginia Company maps and names area *New England*. He especially names Plymouth in 1615 even **before** the Pilgrims arrive in 1620. This effectively puts a British claim on the land where Plymouth became the territorial symbol of English Puritan Protestantism in America and was called *New Canaan*. This Puritan environment was the religious *zeitgeist* nourishing the baker woman's early religious background. Puritanism also was a major influence on the American Protestantism which uniquely shapes the American religious thought.

The Spanish Armada invading England was first spotted sailing into England's Plymouth Sound. Plymouth supplied seven ships to the battle against the Armada. The name *Plymouth* certainly is significant concerning the events leading to freedom from *little horn* domination.

❹
Colonization Complete
With restoration of the monarchy in England under Charles II, the Napoleonic Act was reenacted, old grievances revived, and finally the Dutch Colony of New Netherlands was seized in time of peace (1664) and its capital, New Amsterdam, renamed New York. In the eloquent words of the historian Boorstin ". . . the English [Protestant] flag now waved over an unbroken coast from Canada to the Carolinas." Now even geography was favoring the inevitable restoration of primitive Christianity or the Science of Christianity which the Nazarene himself said "will lead you into all truth." He referred to this coming as "the spirit of truth". The spirit of something is the science of that something. The Second Advent was eventually to appear in the Nation formed by these colonies. Its form would be the *Science of Christianity* or "the spirit of truth" as promised by the Master Christian himself. "Howbeit when he, the Spirit of truth, is come, he will guide you into all truth. . ."(John 16:13) It's messenger would be the *baker* woman with the three measures of meal prophesied by Jesus.

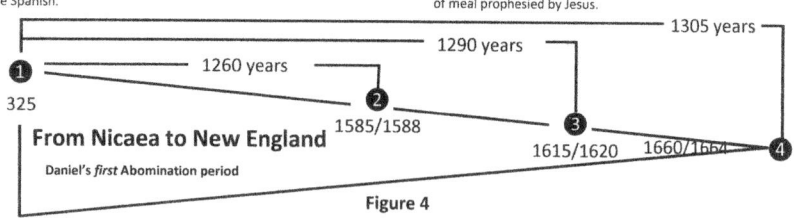

From Nicaea to New England
Daniel's *first* Abomination period

325 ❶ 1260 years ❷ 1585/1588 1290 years ❸ 1615/1620 1660/1664 ❹ 1305 years

Figure 4

Chapter II
From Nicaea to New England

Constantine and the Nicaean Council

1

The nineteenth-century French author Charles Diehl wrote that "by making Christianity a state religion, by multiplying immunities and privileges in its favor, by defending it against heresy, and by multiplying immunities and privileges in its favor, and by extending his protection to it under all circumstances, Constantine gave an altogether different character to the power of the Emperor. Seated among the bishops, as if he were one of them; posing as the accredited guardian of dogma and discipline; intervening in all affairs of the Church; legislating and giving judgment in its name, organizing and directing it, convoking and presiding over its councils; dictating the formulas of faith, Constantine—and *all his successors* [emphasis added] after him, whether orthodox or Ariens—regulated according to one uniform principle the relations of State and Church. This is what came to be called *Caesaropapism,* the despotic authority of the emperor over the church."

In the third volume of his work *History of the Christian Church* (Grand Rapids: William B. Eerdmans Publishing Co.), Philip Schaff writes: "Constantine, the first Christian Caesar, ... was the first representative of the imposing idea of a Christian theocracy, ... and regards church and state as the two arms of one and the same divine government on earth. This idea was more fully developed by his successors, it animated the whole middle age. ... At the same time, however, Constantine stands also as the type of an undiscriminating and harmful conjunction of Christianity with politics. ... Soon after him, Leo the Great, the first representative of consistent, exclusive, universal papacy, advocated even the penalty of death for heresy. ... [Constantine stated the doctrine that] 'Nothing conquers but truth, the victory of truth is love.' But his theory, as Neander observes, contains the germ of the whole system of spiritual despotism, intolerance, and persecution, even to the court of the Inquisition. ... Justin Martyr, Tertullian, and even Lactantius were the first advocates of the principle of freedom of conscience, and maintained against the heathen, that religion was essentially a matter of free will, and could be promoted only be instruction and persuasion, not by outward force. All they say against the persecution of Christians by the heathen applies in full to the persecution of heretics by the church. After the Nicene age all departures from the reigning state-church faith were not only abhorred and excommunicated as religious errors, but were treated also as crimes against the Christian state, and hence were punished with civil penalties; at first with deposition, banishment, confiscations, and, after Theodosius, even with death" (pp. 12, 17, 23, 145).

It is not surprising, however, that the Roman political state evolved in time into Daniel's little horn, or ecclesiastical, state, given the bent of the Roman mind toward the ecclesiastical and religious. Pagels, the distinguished Princeton professor of religion, writes that "for most Romans, political and social obligations were religious—the center of all that they held sacred" (*Adam, Eve, and the Serpent*, 49).

Hutton states in *The Church of the Sixth Century*: "From the point of view of the historian, it is clear that the whole future of Christendom depended upon the acceptance by the Christian nations of a single rational, and logically tenable creed" (56). Maybe so, from the point of view of the historian, but this is a secular view that ignores the early history of the Christian church. Clearly, if Christianity had continued to heal the sick through spiritual means only—as Jesus demanded—this would not be so. The early phenomenal growth was a direct result of this practice. Gibbon states in *Decline and Fall of the Roman Empire* that "the scanty and suspicious materials of ecclesiastical history seldom enables us to dispel the cloud that hangs over the first age of the church" (347). This cloud, no doubt, obscures the devastating forces that led to the fall of true Christianity. We know that Gnosticism and scholasticism played its part. Gradually Aesculapian medicine usurped this practice by the Christians, and by the date of the Nicene Council, it had essentially come to an end and from that date the "Christian" church fell under the medical practice of the Romans. This practice grew out of Greek paganism, was Aesculapian entirely, and was directly opposite from that mighty force that had built the "real" Christian church. Thus a modern Aesculapian priesthood gradually evolved in which faith in drugs, vaccines, and other non-spiritual icons replaced Jesus' great promise and proof that God heals disease directly. This is one part of the little horn that Martin Luther did not purge. However, in some of his *Table Talks* we learn that he did practice purely Christian healing very successfully in a number of cases. One document relates that he actually brought the gentle Melanchthon back from the brink of death. These practitioners may well have noble, gentle, and kind sympathies. That is a credit to their personal character, but it misses the point. The point is that we have substituted matter for Spirit as the healer of the sick. A testimony to the nobility of *materia medica* practitioners when they have witnessed Christian healing was described in Eddy's work *The First Church of Christ, Scientist and Miscellany*. She writes: "About the year 1869, I was wired to attend the patient of a distinguished M.D., the late Dr. Davis of Manchester, N.H. The patient was pronounced dying of pneumonia, and was breathing at intervals in agony. Her physician, who stood by her bedside, declared that she could not live. On seeing her immediately restored by me without material aid, he asked earnestly if I had a work describing my system of healing. When answered in the negative, he urged me immediately to write a book which should explain to the world my curative system of metaphysics. In the ranks of the M.D.'s are noble men and women, and I love them" (105). Thus, she wrote *Science and Health with Key to the Scriptures*.

It is also not obvious that the Nicene Creed is either rational or logically tenable. It appears as an outgrowth of a period where polytheism was not unacceptable. As to the ready acceptance of a tritheistic deity, maybe one shouldn't be too surprised. Various pagan religions over the millennia have embraced a tritheistic deity. Brahmanism is a good example, but there are many others. The first law of Moses' Commandments hardly embraces the notion of three gods in one God or of a tritheistic deity. The Nicaean syncretism grew out of the inability to understand the difference between Jesus the *Son* of God and Jesus *as* God. Paul's message to the Corinthians itself should settle the question. In I Corinthians 15:28, he writes that "when all things shall be subdued unto him [Jesus] then shall the Son also himself be subject unto him that put all things under him, that *God* [emphasis added] may be all in all." How can any phase of God be subject unto itself?

If the violation of the First Commandment had any meaning whatsoever for Athanasius, he certainly had no trouble violating the sixth one since he was more than willing to have anyone who disagreed with his speculative creed put to death! Interestingly enough, Constantine, the Christian emperor who underwrote this creed, believed in the god Apollo until his death, but at the same time claimed allegiance to the Judeo-Christian God. So much for his strict understanding of the First Commandment!

Given the fact that Christian healing (healing by the power of God as Jesus healed and instructed all his followers to heal) was the potent factor that led to the early spectacular success of real Christianity, it is not difficult to understand why real Christian healing essentially ended in the time period of the Nicaean era. It could hardly be a coincidence that these two events coincided. Jesus warned: "Beware of the leaven of the Scribes and Pharisees." What else was this leaven but man-made theology replacing the healing science-divine of Jesus of Nazareth? This divine Science had been declining in human thought in the three hundred years preceding Nicaea, and Christian healing declined accordingly, but this council was the final denouement and marked the beginning of a long, dark era, culminating in the Dark Ages. Imagine an emperor who supposedly had adopted Christianity, but had not totally surrendered all Roman mythology, presiding over an ecumenical council that was to put forth the most fundamental theological dogma for the future Christian churches! This emperor had a choice between the theology of Arias or Athanasius. His polytheistic Roman mind had no problem there. He chose the one that hinted at polytheism. This is not to suggest that either one of them was scientific theology, but it certainly shows what a pagan's natural inclinations can do to Christian theology if he has the authority to influence it.

This period of 325 A.D. marked the first of, or beginning of, Daniel's abomination of desolation. This is the period when the last of Christian healing as Jesus commanded of his followers to practice disappeared and was replaced by the pagan Greek Aesculapian medicine, which prevails to this day. This is not to denigrate in any way the kindness and compassion of the best of modern doctors, or especially their surgical skills, but what book, chapter and verse in the New Testament instructs the Christian to abandon his Master's strict instruction concerning Christian healing as he did it? Jesus was in no way ignorant of Aesculapian medical practice. It was in the culture. It surrounded him! This is the period when pagan Rome declared Christianity the official state religion. This is the period when the half-converted Roman emperor decided the fundamental theological doctrine of what constituted the Christ and how this related to the Godhead. This is the period when man-made theology began to replace biblical truth in direct disobedience to Jesus' command to beware the leaven of the Scribes and Pharisees. This period marked the beginning of the time when death was the penalty for not complying with the theology and teachings of the coming Latin Church, and, according to Jon Foxe's *Book of Martyrs* (Grand Rapids: Zondervan Publishing House), caused the slaughter of more than sixty million individuals for non-compliance. This is the period when Daniel's little horn was beginning to transform Rome from the most powerful political empire in history into the most powerful ecclesiastical tyranny in history, resulting in such events as the horrific Spanish Inquisition. This must be the period of which Jesus spoke when he said to "work while it is day for the night cometh when no man can work." Was this a prophecy of the Dark Ages? No question!

A profoundly important historical irony is that Luther's Reformation not only inaugurated the Protestant movement but also ultimately resulted in the political liberation of the Latin Church itself and thus freed it from the little horn involvement. Although the Latin Church is structured today similarly to what it was historically, it is now a strictly religious denomination like other religious denominations, with its adherents legally free to choose its theology or some other theology. Even absolute Christian truth, if legally enforced, would lose its power to bless. Daniel's little horn symbolized such a marriage, a marriage that ultimately had to end in divorce!

The date of 325, chosen as the beginning date of Daniel's first abomination—commencing the first historical time interval of a time, times, and half a time—was not arbitrary. All of Daniel's time intervals are concerned with the gradual evolution of Rome from a political into an ecclesiastical entity (i.e., the origin and subsequent development of the little horn followed by historical events leading out of little horn control of the entire Christian church).

Schaff writes that "Constantine, the *first* [emphasis added] Christian Caesar, … was the first representative of the imposing idea of a Christian theocracy … and regards church and state as the two arms of one and the same divine government on earth. This idea was more fully developed by his successors, it animated the whole middle age" *(History of Christianity,* 12). Of course, his landmark identity in this process was the 325 A.D. Nicaean Council. Although Eusebios and others proclaimed this a great victory for Christianity, was it really? Read Schaff again: "At the same time, however, Constantine stands also as the type of an indiscriminating and harmful conjunction of Christianity with politics. This [Constantine's] theory [about love, truth, and conquering] as Neander observes, 'Contains the germ of the whole system of spiritual despotism, intolerance, and persecution, even to the court of the Inquisition'" (12, 145).

He certainly lays the groundwork for Leo the Great, characterized by Schaff:

> Soon after him [Constantine,] Leo the Great, the first representative of consistent, exclusive, universal papacy, advocated even the penalty of death for heresy, ... Justin Martyr, Tertullian, and even Tactantius were the first advocates of the principle of freedom of conscience, and maintained, against the heathen, that religion was essentially a matter of free will, and could be promoted only by instruction and persuasion, not by outward force. All they say against the persecution of Christians by the heathen applies in full to the persecution of heretics by the church. After the Nicene age all departures from the reigning state-church faith were not only abhorred and excommunicated as religious errors, but treated also as crimes against the Christian state, and hence were punished with civil penalties at first with deposition, banishment, confiscation and after Theodocius, even with death. *(History of the Christian Church,* 139, 145)

Was our beloved Master knowingly putting forth a double entendre when he gave the "keys to the kingdom" to Peter, or was he really referring to Peter or to a church-state claiming to be Peter's incarnation, figuratively speaking? Was he prophesying the claims of the perpetual Roman bishop to decree salvation or damnation upon his subjects? If the Bishop of Rome really had this power, he held, indeed, the keys to an individual's heaven or hell! Certainly Jesus saw the coming Dark Ages growing out of this presumption of such power. Why, otherwise, would he have urged his followers to "work while it is day for the night [Dark Ages] cometh when no man can work?" Could the Prophet-of-prophets have possibly not foreseen what historians now call the darkest period in human history? Although this dark period began roughly at the beginning of the seventh century and continued more or less for half a millennium, it came about as the inevitable product of the birth and development of Daniel's little horn. It certainly is no mere play upon words that the Latin institution referred to itself as the *Holy See*. Daniel gives special symbolic meaning to the "eye" of the little horn.

Since the birth of Jesus occurred circa 4 B.C., the First Nicene Council was three hundred and twenty-nine years removed from that event. Christian healing was largely proscribed at this council and the seeds of the state religion thoroughly planted, watered, and fertilized. The ante-Nicene form of congregational church structure was for all practical purposes relegated to the historical scrap heap. This was Caesar's day.

The Great Armada

2

The defeat of the Spanish Armada, although chiefly the victory of the British Navy, was partially due to natural sea impediments. It is as if Providence was reaching forth to prevent the little horn from capturing England, and most especially, ultimately dominating the North American continent. One of these impediments was strange sea currents with which the Spaniards were not acquainted. What is of particular irony, we now know, is that these sea currents were caused by Gulf Stream phenomena originating in the New World. It is as if a hand across the sea reached forth with a "thus far and no farther" directive. Although eventually appearing on the North American continent, the final deliverance from the little horn's Spanish legion was determined by the Battle of Bloody Marsh in the colony of Georgia, where General Edward Oglethorpe drove them into the southern part of the New World. It is indeed an irony that the nationality clinging the longest to Arianism should eventually become the most despotic people in cruel defense of Athanasius's tritheism, and it would be that branch of the Roman Empire—turned little horn—that would be the agent to attempt to bring the little horn to the North American colonies. These are the people who evolved the most fanatical of the religious orders and who literally were historical revisionists who perfected the use of the dialectic. This was the nation whose conquistadors brought the little horn to the New World where, in the colony of Georgia, its defeat at the historic Battle of Bloody Marsh meant that the United States would be Protestant and would not therefore fall under the tyranny of the little horn.

> The summer of 1588 was marked by a succession of gales of unprecedented violence. The damaged and weakened Spanish ships, which were from the first greatly undermanned in sailors, were unable to contend with the storms. It is not possible to give the details of the disasters which overtook them. Of the total number of the vessels originally collected for the invasion of England one-half, if not more, perished, and the crews of those which escaped were terribly diminished by scurvy and starvation. (*Encyclopedia Britannica*, 11th ed., s.v. "Armada, The")

Plymouth
3

Perhaps no other event in American history incites a patriotic thinker—concerning her destiny—than the Plymouth experience! These words, written in 1802 by John Quincy Adams, illustrate the point:

> When the persecuted companions of Robinson, exiles from their native land, anxiously sued for the privilege of removing a thousand leagues more distant to an untried soil, a rigorous climate and a savage wilderness, for the sake of reconciling their sense of religious duty with their affections for their country, few, perhaps none of them formed a conception of what would be within two centuries the result of their undertaking. When the jealous and niggardly policy of

their British sovereign denied them even that humblest of requests, and instead of liberty would barely consent to promise connivance, neither he nor they might be aware that they were laying the foundations of a power, and that he was sowing the seeds of a spirit, which in less than two hundred years would stagger the throne of his descendants, and shake his united kingdoms to the centre. (New York Historical Society; Pilgrim Hall Museum, Plymouth)

The writer would presumptuously add to the above passage: "Commence a movement whereby a government, for the first time in history, would provide the proper secular conditions to shepherd the coming of the Second Advent, an event even more staggering!" Perhaps the reader will be patient and read the following poem by Felicia Dorothea Hemans, written in 1808 (London: Oxford University Press, 1914):

> The breaking waves dash'd high
> On a stern and rock-bound coast,
> And the woods against a stormy sky
> Their giant branches toss'd.
> And the heavy night hung dark
> The hills and waters o'er,
> When a band of exiles moor'd their bark
> On the wild New England shore.
>
> Not as the conqueror comes,
> They, the true-hearted, came;
> Not with the roll of the stirring drums,
> And the trumpet that sings of fame;
> Not as the flying come,
> In silence and in fear:
> They shook the depths of the desert gloom
> With their hymns of lofty cheer.

Amidst the storm they sang,
And the stars heard, and the sea:
And the sounding aisles of the dim woods rang
To the anthem of the free.
The ocean eagle soared
From his nest by the white wave's foam,
And the rocking pines of the forest roared,
This was their welcome home.

What sought they thus afar?
Bright jewels from the mine?
The wealth of seas, the spoils of war?
They sought a faith's pure shrine.
Ay, call it holy ground,
The soil which first they trod:
They have left un-stained what there they found,
Freedom to worship God.

In *The Pilgrim Fathers* (Boston: Merrymount Press, 1937), Samuel Eliot Morison described the Pilgrims as "a simple people, inspired by an ardent faith in God, a dauntless courage in danger, a boundless resourcefulness in the face of difficulties, an impregnable fortitude in adversity: thus they have in some measure become the spiritual ancestors of all Americans." Could Daniel's biblical arithmology have possibly missed such an event as the predestined Pilgrim event? Hardly! Daniel's biblical arithmology has not failed to date the historical time-appearing of every single vital event necessary to prepare the way for the Second Advent!

Colonization Complete
4

In his work *Plymouth and the Pilgrims* (Boston: Houghton Mifflin, 1920), Arthur Lord writes: "The Pilgrim movement can be but imperfectly understood if treated as an isolated event in the world's history, without reference to the conditions which preceded it and make its success possible. Looking at it broadly, it was part of a great world movement, and its relation to that movement must be considered in order to understand its meaning and appreciate the result" (1).

Lord also writes: "No fact has had a greater influence on the history of civilization, as stated by an eminent scholar than that the land of the globe is divided into two great sections, the mass of Europe, Asia and Africa on the one side and the two Americas on the other, and that one of these worlds remained unknown to the other till only 400 years ago" (ibid.).

New England Puritanism was historically significant and nurtured the woman of the Second Advent. But more fundamentally, the forged chain-links of the little horn could hardly have been broken without this worldwide phenomenon. The enslaving, freedom-impeding forces of Old Europe were simply too strong!

Second Abomination Period

Attila and Leo 1

The death of Attila and the sacking of Rome was reflective of the beginning of the metamorphosis in which Rome was moving from a mighty political power into her new role as a dictatorial ecclesiastical empire, the period of the reign of the Little Horn., The total transformation was to be a little less than a century and a half from this date. The emperor Justinian was yet to attempt to restore the entire Roman Empire. Tribonian's distilled Roman law inadvertently played a part in the complete transformation; although that wasn't Justinian's intent. Even the sacking of totalitarian *political* Rome was clearly symbolic of the ultimate arrival of a government "of the people, by the people and for the people." It was under this kind of government that the baker woman with the three measures of meal was to usher in the Second Advent! Daniel's *time, times, and a half time,* added to this Attila death-date, takes us to a date when a treaty ultimately concedes the southern portion of North America to the British colonizers who were destined to found this new government of, for, and by the people.

Treaty of Utrecht

"The Treaty of Utrecht is second to none in importance to English history. Its provisions were a most potent factor in assisting the expansion of England's colonial empire. . ." These are the words of the distinguished eleventh edition of the *Encyclopedia Britannica* : *Under this treaty Louis xiv essentially conceded France's claim to North America. England obtained possession of Newfoundland, Nova Scotia, Hudson's Bay territory and more.* Louis also recognized the <u>Protestant</u> succession in England! In short, a very important link in the concatenation of events leading to Protestant (not *Little Horn*) control of North America.

Battle of Bloody Marsh

It was a threat from Spain. . .that led to the organization of the last colony, Georgia. The Battle of Bloody Marsh ended the great Spanish plan to throw the colonists out of Georgia and ultimately to take control of all the colonies. This decisive English victory represented the last major Spanish offensive into Georgia and thence into the colonies. Caroline Couper Lovell writes in *The Golden Isles of Georgia* "Because of its far-reaching importance, the battle of Bloody Marsh ranks as one of the decisive battles of the world, and St. Simon's has been called the Thermopylae of the Southern Provinces." "The deliverance of Georgia from the Spaniards," said Whitfield, the famous preacher, is such as can not be paralleled but by some instance out of the Old Testament." Sir Thomas Carlyle, observer-genius, of significant events in human history opined of this battle that it was to determine whether the colonies went Spanish [Latin or *little horn*) or English [protestant]. "For this great victory and the far reaching effect it had on the American colonists General Oglethorpe received the thanks of the Colonial Governors of New York, New Jersey, Pennsylvania, Maryland, Virginia and North Carolina."—American Historical Society

Wings of the Eagle

The woman was prophesied to take the wings of the eagle to protect her in the wilderness. (Revelation: 12:14. Surely this document (unique in the history of the whole world for the protection of individual rights of conscience) was the long awaited *legal* setting for the Second Advent. Her "place" in the wilderness is obviously to illuminate it with light. But this could only be done if her Church could be established under a legal system conducive to the rights of the individual to own his individual consciousness free of even attempted legal interference

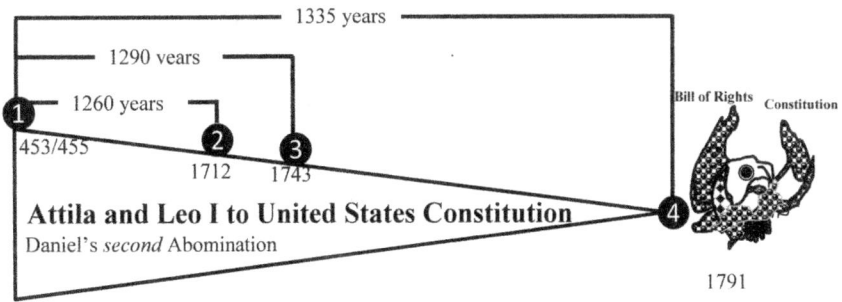

Attila and Leo I to United States Constitution

Daniel's *second* Abomination

1335 years
1290 years
1260 years
453/455
1712
1743
Bill of Rights   Constitution
1791

Figure 5

Chapter III
Attila and Leo I to the United States Constitution

Attila and Leo I
1

Attila the Hun and Pope Leo I dominated this period. According to the *Encyclopedia Britannica Eleventh Edition* (s.v. "Attila"), "when Pope Leo I, at the head of a deputation of Roman senators, appeared in his [Attila's] camp on the banks of the Muncie, entreating him not to pursue his victorious career to the gates of Rome, he yielded to their entreaties and consented. ... As he himself jokingly said: he knew how to conquer men, but the Lion and the wolf (Leo and Lupus) were too strong for him."

Edward Gibbon says, "The barbarian monarch listened with favorable, and even respectful, attention. ... No further expeditions to Italy were undertaken by Attila who died suddenly in 453" (*Decline and Fall*, 1097). Again from Gibbon (ibid., 1095): "The savage destroyer *undesignedly* [emphasis added] laid the foundations of a republic which revived, in the feudal state of Europe, the art and spirit of commercial industry." It is interesting to note how the death of the ruthless barbarian marked another significant date in the growing strength of the little horn—the developing transformation of Rome from a mighty secular power into an almost almighty ecclesiastical one.

There always seems to be some element of mysticism in the zeitgeist of ancient Rome. Was Attila really "jokingly" talking in his reference to Leo the Great and the lupine foster-mother of Romulus and Remus? Gibbon writes: "When Attila declared his resolution of carrying his victorious arms to the gates of Rome, he was admonished by his friends, as well as by his enemies, that Alaric had not long survived the conquest of the eternal city. His mind, superior to real danger, was assaulted by imaginary terrors nor could he escape the influence of superstition, which had been so often subservient to his designs. The pressing eloquence of Leo I, his majestic aspect and sacerdotal robes, excited the veneration of Attila for the spiritual father of the Christians. The apparition of the two apostles St. Peter and St. Paul who menaced the barbarian with instant death [as he supposed] if he rejected the prayer of their successor" (*Decline and Fall*, 1098). Here is manifested the mysticism underlying the whole phenomenon of the little horn development.

In *History of the Christian Church*, Schaff writes: "Besides thus shaping the polity and doctrine of the church, Leo did immortal service to the city of Rome, in twice rescuing it from destruction. When Attila, king of the Huns, the 'Scourge of God' ... was seriously threatening the capital of the world ... [Leo] ventured into the hostile camp, and by his venerable form, his remonstrances and his gifts changed the wild heathen's purpose. ... The first Leo and the first Gregory are the two greatest bishops of Rome in the first six centuries Leo thought and acted as an absolute: Gregory as first among the patriarchs but both under the full conviction that they were the successors of Peter the papal power had been rather favoured than hindered in its growth by the imbecility of the latest emperors. Now, to a certain extent, it stepped into the imperial vacancy, and the successor [the little horn] became, in the mind of the Western nations, sole heir of the old Roman imperial succession" (321).

It is significant that the only popes anointed "the Great" were Leo and Gregory. It is especially significant since Leo commenced, and Gregory completed, the papal archetypes of the little horn, i.e., the clerical influence and power causing the Roman Empire's metamorphism from a political into an ecclesiastical empire as Daniel predicted. Leo the Great saved the real estate for the little horn. Although as Gibbon has it, Attila played his part even here as "the savage destroyer undesignedly laid the foundations of a republic which revived, in the feudal state of Europe, the art and spirit of commercial industry" (Gibbon, *Decline and Fall*, 1095).

Unquestionably Attila and Leo, via a strange chemistry, effected the little horn's first major rise to power. The degeneracy of the emperors no doubt allowed the clergy to eventually rule the empire. Daniel's figure of Rome with the feet of iron mixed with clay was graphically accurate. Historically the clay began to dominate the iron. The clergy were waiting!

Treaty of Utrecht
2

The Treaty of Utrecht concluded the European War of Spanish Succession. Had that war been concluded with Spanish victory, the country of the infamous Spanish Inquisition would have dominated the Teutonic nations, although France would have been the immediate benefactor.

> France's plan for a great empire in America was now taking shape and there, as in Europe, a deadly struggle with England was inevitable. Frontenac planned attacks upon New England and encouraged a ruthless border warfare that involved many horrors. ...
>
> LaSalle's expedition had aroused the French to the importance of the Mississippi, and they soon had a bold plan to occupy it, to close in from the rear on the English on the Atlantic coast, seize their colonies and even deport the colonists. When the Treaty of Utrecht was made in 1713 France admitted defeat in America. (*Encyclopedia Britannica*, 11th ed., s.v. "Utrecht, Treaty of")

The little horn law would have dominated Europe, and the American colonies would be under the ecclesiastical power of the little horn. Both France and Spain were little-horn agents in the New World. Luther's nucleonic explosion, which had its loudest reverberation in the New World, would have been less than an echo if either one of these powers had prevailed.

Another vitally necessary circumstance growing out of this treaty was the guarantee from Louis XIV that he would give no more aid and support to the Stuarts. This has to be extremely important since the Stuarts were determined to make England Roman Catholic. In other words, it was recognition from Catholic France of Protestant succession in England. The last Stuart on the throne of England was Anne (daughter of James II). She was succeeded in 1714 by George I, and this was the beginning of the Protestant Hanover, later calling itself the "House of Windsor" line that still sits on the English throne. If France had been successful, our great Pilgrim and Puritan colonies from which she who ushered in the Second Advent came forth would have been wiped out. Such was the intention of Louis XIV, the great Sun King of France.

The recognition of the Protestant succession in England eventually led indirectly to New England Puritanism. From this evolved the Protestant zeitgeist of the United States. It permeated the thinking of our founding fathers, even the Episcopalian ones. The Church of England was guaranteed the freedom from Rome (the little horn) initiated by Henry VIII. The Stuarts were forever removed from the future history of England and therefore prevented from fixing their imprimatur upon the New World. Ultimately, even the Latin church benefited. The American doctrine of separation of church and state eventually affected Europe and played its part in freeing the Latin church to become a religion of choice, and not a product of state identity. Lord has this to say of the Sun King:

> He was a bigot and a persecutor. ... Louis was
> a devout Catholic in spite of his sins, and was true
> to the interests of the Pope. ... He detested all re-
> bellion from the spiritual authority of the popes;

he hated both heresy and schism. [He was devoted] to the Catholic Church ... In Louis' reign the State and Church were firmly knit together. ... As early as 1666 the King was urged, and long before the Edict of Nantes was revoked the Protestants had been subjected to humiliation and annoyance ... from 1685. The poor, unoffending Protestants filled the prisons and dyed the scaffolds with their blood. They were prohibited under the severest penalties from the exercise of their religion; their ministers were exiled, their children were baptized in the Catholic faith, their property was confiscated, and all attempts to flee the country were punished by the galleys. Two millions of people were disfranchised two hundred thousand perished by the executioners or in prisons, or in the galleys. (*Beacon Lights of History,* vol. 8: 258-259, 279-280)

This military defeat of the little horn surrogate secured the rise of that which was ultimately to destroy the power of the little horn to dominate the religious practice of the world. In this, the scattered power of the holy people would be restored. The War of Spanish Succession was a war fought not only in Europe, but also in colonial North America, where the conflict became known to the English colonies as Queen Anne's War. This war was the second in a series of four French and Indian wars fought between France and England in North America for control of the continent and was the counterpart of the war of the Spanish Succession in Europe. It was the American phase of the War of the Spanish Succession.

There is little doubt that this war laid the foundation for the Celto-Anglo-Saxon domination of the new world. In this war, England gained most of the advantage. The decline of the little horn Spain as a major power on the European continent was completed. Arising initially out of French and Indian raids on British settlements along the New York and New England borders with Canada, it was the American phase of the War of the Spanish Succession.

The name "Queen Anne's War" is only used in the United States. In Canada, Britain, and France, this war is simply considered a theatre of the War of the Spanish Succession.

A different outcome of this war, both on the European continent and in North America, would have been a decisive victory for the little horn. The North American continent would have been under Latin and not Anglo Saxon Protestant law, and the great American experiment clearing the way for the Second Advent would have remained an unfulfilled hope. That was not to be! Spain was the mother of the cruelest of all the inquisitors. Suppose this surrogate of the little horn had won that battle! But the Spanish would make one more attempt on the colonies. This last attempt would be thwarted by the Battle of Bloody Marsh. This attempt occurred in 1742. It was an event of overwhelming significance. Some historians have rated General James Edward Oglethorpe second only to George Washington in importance to American history, There is a reason for this: Spain and England both were intent to possess what is now the American territory. The Spanish had already established military outposts and missionary operations as far up the Atlantic coast as Beaufort, South Carolina, and actually claimed territory still farther into Cape Hatteras, North Carolina. In a showdown at the Battle at Bloody Marsh off the coast of Georgia, Oglethorpe defeated the Spanish against overwhelming odds.

The Battle of Bloody Marsh
3

This battle took place during a Spanish invasion of present-day Georgia. The battle was virtually a miraculous victory for English troops under General Oglethorpe, given the incredible odds they faced. The battle was a particular of the War of Jenkins Ear. On October 30, 1739, Great Britain declared war on Spain. Spain and Great Britain had been disputing the border between Georgia and La Florida. General Oglethorpe led the colonization of

Georgia by Great Britain. The colony was founded to halt the spread of the Spanish into the colonies. General Oglethorpe was commander and chief of all British forces in South Carolina and Georgia.

Because of the critical part a little-known battle played in saving the North American continent from Spain, and consequently little horn domination, the following observations by distinguished scholarly men are here added, from the first volume of *Georgia's Landmarks, Memorials and Legends* by L.L. Knight:

> Bloody Marsh: Where a battle was fought in which Spain lost a Continent.—Between the lighthouse at St. Simon's and the old citadel of Frederica there stretches a low plain on which was staged a war drama, the far–reaching effect of which upon the subsequent fortunes of America hardly admits of a parallel in the history of the New World. Here on July 7, 1742, was fought the historic battle of Bloody Marsh. To quote an authority whose opinion is universally accepted, Thomas Carlyle, "half the world was hidden in embryo under it:" and this wisest seer and clearest thinker of the nineteenth century adds: "The Yankee nation itself was involved, the greatest phenomenon of these ages." The renowned George Whitefield (1714-1770), the renowned cleric who helped his friend John Wesley found the Methodist Church and of whom Lord Chesterfield said, "He is the greatest orator I ever heard and I cannot conceive of a greater" declared of Georgia's deliverance from the Spaniards at this time was to be paralleled "Only by some instance out of the Old Testament." Said he: "Certain it is that this battle, though well nigh forgotten, is one of the most glorious and decisive in the annals of our country. It determined that North America should be left to the exploitation of the Anglo–Saxon, the Celtic and the Teutonic races. Had success attended the

Spaniards they would have advanced upon the more northern settlements." To quote an eminent jurist of this state, "General Oglethorpe received from the governors of New York, New Jersey, Pennsylvania, Maryland, Virginia and North Carolina a special letter, congratulating him on his success and expressing gratitude to the Supreme Governor of Nations for placing the affairs of the colonies under the direction of a General so well qualified for the important trust." In the ancient Spanish burial ground near Frederica lie the remains of some of the hapless victims who fell in this engagement, but the sacred area is choked with briars and brambles while, amid the damp undergrowth, hisses the vengeful snake. The disappearance of the Spanish flag, on January 1, 1799, from the whole upper half of the Western Hemisphere, when the independence of Cuba was recognized by the government of Madrid, merely served to record the final issues of the great victory achieved by Oglethorpe when, with a force of six hundred men, he inaugurated the era of Spain's downfall and gave the whole continent of North America to English civilization.

Caroline Couper Lovell wrote in her *Golden Isles of Georgia* that Bloody Marsh ranks as one of the decisive battles of the world. Carolyn Cobb, granddaughter of one of Georgia's distinguished governors, said to the author concerning this victory: "Little did Carlyle know; that the way was being made possible for the appearing of the Discoverer and Founder of Christian Science—the Science of the Christ, Mary Baker Eddy." She was well aware of the implication and said that "the decisive Battle of Bloody Marsh determining, we know, for all time the future religious freedom of this country." Note how all of the distinguished commentators saw it as the battle to decide the religious future of North America and, by implication, of the whole world. What is of staggering interest is that they perceived the prophetic implications at the time, while Daniel foresaw it thousands of years before; although he was not aware of the specific nature of the event, he clearly knew the date!

The Hon. Richard D. Meader of Brunswick, Georgia writes: "The entire population of Georgia at the same time had 68,000, North Carolina 80,000 and Virginia 275,000. In 1742 Georgia probably did not number more than 4,000 inhabitants, so that we have the spectacle of a small army of 6,550 men, less than a modern regiment defending more than 300,000 people against the attack of a powerful enemy without any assistance from those people. Assuming that Georgia's population was 4,000 in 1742, it is not probable that the adult male population was more than one third that number, so that we see another unusual spectacle, that of one half the entire male population being engaged in one force, a proportion which I doubt has ever been equal in the world's history. Had this small army of 650 men been killed or captured by the Spaniards, there could have been no effective resistance from the other parts of the colony, and Georgia as an English colony would have ceased to exist, while South Carolina and the more northern colonies would have had to fight for their existence. Oglethorpe knowing the overpowering strength of the Spanish and his own weakness realized the desperate straits he was in and made repeated but fruitless calls for additional troops upon the more northern colonies. Finally realizing that he must rely upon what force he had, in the face of great and impending dangers he wrote those brave and memorable words which appear above his name on the monument that we are dedicating today. Embedded in the monument in a near table of bronze on which the following inscription is lettered: 'We are resolved not to suffer defeat. We will rather die like Leonidas and his Spartans, if we but protect Georgia and the Carolinas and the rest of the Americans from desolation.' —James Edward Oglethorpe ... Fort Frederica: 1735—On the west side of St. Simon's Island, at a point which commands the entrance to the Altamaha River, stands an ancient pile, the origin of which can be traced to the days of Oglethorpe. It is the oldest of Georgia's historic ruins. Some of the very guns which were used to expel the Spaniards may be seen upon its moss-covered ramparts: and not only the earliest but the bravest memories of Colonial times cluster about its dismantled walls. Except for the part which it played in checking the haughty arrogance of Madrid, an altogether different sequel might have been given to the subsequent history of North America, for here it was that the Castilian power in the western hemisphere was for the first time challenged and the march of Spain toward the North halted by an overwhelming victory for the English colonies. ... Time has spared only the barest remnant of the ancient citadel which saved the continent of North America from Spanish domination. (Knight, *Georgia's Landmarks, Memorials and Legends,* vol. 2)

On the public monument marking the battle are these words of Oglethorpe himself:

"We are resolved not to suffer defeat-
We will rather die like Leonidas and his Spartans
If we can but protect Georgia and Carolina and the
Rest of the Americans from desolations."

Wings of the Eagle
4

The late Hon. Samuel J. Erwin Jr., a recognized expert on constitutional law, had this to say: "If any provision of the Constitution can be said to be more precious than the others, it is the provision of the First Amendment which undertakes to separate church and state by keeping government's hands out of religion and by denying to any and all religious denominations any advantage from getting control of public policy or the public purse."

Schaff writes:

> History had taught the framers of the Constitution that persecution is useless as well as hateful and that it has its root in the unholy alliance of religion with politics. … The constitutional provision of the United States in regard to religion is the last outcome of the Reformation in its effect upon toleration and freedom, not foreseen or dreamed of by the Reformers, but inevitably resulting from their revolt against papal tyranny. It has grown on Protestant soil with the hearty support of all sects and parties. It cuts the chief root of papal and any other persecution, and makes it legally impossible. … No part of the federal constitution is so generally accepted and so heartily approved as that which guaranties religious liberty, the most sacred and most important of all liberties. (*History of the Christian Church*, 82)

The writer, while visiting Independence Hall on Bicentennial Day and gazing upon the Liberty Bell, noticed the infamous crack in this symbol of human freedom. Some have suggested that this crack symbolizes that slavery was, in effect, accepted in the Constitution. Perhaps so, but slavery has been abolished. To the writer, this crack symbolizes a matter addressed by Benjamin

Rush, the signer of the Declaration of Independence and personal physician to George Washington:

> Unless we put medical freedom into the Constitution, the time will come when medicine will organize into an undercover dictatorship. ... To restrict the art of healing to one class of men and deny equal privileges to others will constitute the Bastille of medical science. All such laws are un-American and despotic and have no place in a republic. ... The Constitution of this republic should make special privilege for medical freedom as well as religious freedom. (*Letters*, 475)

Unfortunately this was not done, and the famous doctor's prediction has come about. The Aesculapian medicine of ancient pagan Greece underlies the *legal* medical practice in the United States and on boards of health and so on to make the final decisions as to an individual's medical rights, and these decisions are generally upheld by courts and judges. This practice of medicine is considered the final authority in our legal system. For those individuals who do not consider Aesculapian medicine their choice, too bad, the Bastille has spoken! If someone deceases while under a non-Aesculapian method, the press makes much ado out of it and argues that under proper treatment the patient would have survived; on the other hand, if someone deceases under Aesculapian treatment, the comment is "well, they did all they could."

The writer is convinced that this egregious injustice will eventually be corrected, cleansing symbolically our great Constitution of the intolerable defect of not having a freedom of medical choice amendment. This is the only serious and important tyranny not cleansed by Luther's Reformation. But, as has been pointed out earlier in this work, in his *Table Talk,* one reads that Luther did some remarkable healings by spiritual means alone. It is recorded that he even raised the gentle Melanchthon from the dead!

Historically, mandatory Aesculapian medicine was forced into Christendom at the time of the Nicaean Council, when Jesus' method of Christian healing by the power of God had largely ceased in spite of the fact that his first command was to heal in this manner. Healing by material means was the medicine in the kingdom of the little horn.

Third Abomination Period

 Justinian's Distilled Roman Law

Justinian's distilled Roman law formed the *horn* or legal power of the ecclesiastical beast that was to reign over the long night. "By the oppressive laws of Justinian the adversaries of the church were made the enemies of the state. .it affords an unfavorable prejudice that his theology should form a very prominent feature of his portrait . . . his Code, and even more especially his novels, confirm and enlarge the privileges of the clergy; and in every dispute between a monk and a layman, the partial judge was inclined to pronounce that truth and innocence and justice were always on the side of the church." So writes Gibbon in *The Decline and Fall of the Roman Empire*.

Bill of Rights

The great American Bill of Rights, a document historically inconceivable, is born! The first Amendment with its focus on separation of Church and state and its guarantee of religious freedom freed the Land of the Second Advent from the oppression of the Latin or *Little horn* law. It must be remembered that Europe and, to a much smaller degree, even England, in spite of Henry VIII was more or less influenced but definitely not governed by the nature of this law as it relates to religious freedom. It had a stranglehold on Europe, though, until Luther and the Reformation.

 Birth of Mary Baker Eddy

The way was now cleared for the birth of the messenger of the Second Advent. The atmospheric *zeit geist* for this appearing did not exist until the world <u>finally</u>, throughout its long history, experienced such an atmosphere. Historians and pundits constantly marvel at this "document of rights," but little do they realize what it <u>really</u> means. The nation that formed it is truly in the *new world*. The year 1821 is significant for major breakthroughs that would have profound effect on the coming century. It also is the birth year of discoverers whose work would penetrate the depths of natural science and modern engineering. The seminal *zeit geist* had arrived! The prophet Daniel made perfectly clear that phenomena of this kind would occur simultaneously with the period of the Second Advent. A long distance from what the *little horn* did to Galileo!

Discovery of Christian Science

Chapter 12 of Daniel speaks of "wonders" and then the question about when they should begin. The first answer is the *time, times, and an half time* or 1260years. Then an even larger blessing in 1290 years, or 30 years later, and finally the ultimate blessing 1335 years or 45 years beyond that. (Daniel 12:7, 11-12) Certainly Christian Science is the ultimate blessing. Blessed indeed is he that waiteth for the 45 years. 1866 ushered in the Second Advent!

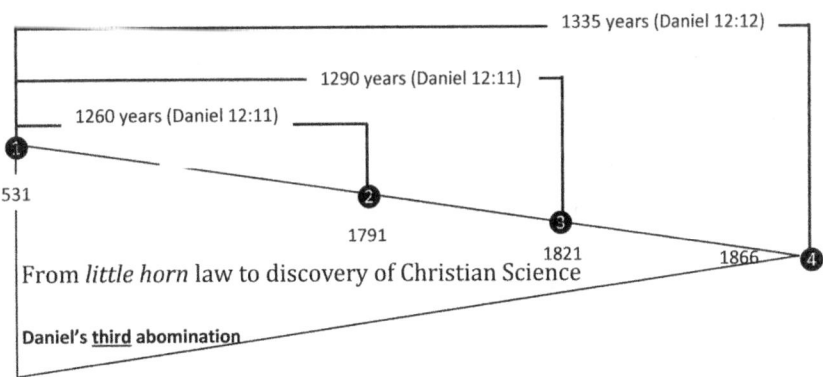

From *little horn* law to discovery of Christian Science

Figure 6

Chapter IV
From Little Horn Law to Discovery of Christian Science

Justinian's Distilled Roman Law
1

In *Beacon Lights of History,* John Lord writes that the papal dominion "was peculiar and unique, a great spiritual government usurping the attributes of other governments, as predicted by Daniel [7:23-25] and, at first benignant, ripening into a gloomy tyranny—a tyranny so unscrupulous and grasping as to become finally, [centuries later], in the eyes of Luther, an evil power."

Note also how these Daniel verses noted above refer to the little horn's use of law for his own purposes.

The *legal* birth of the little horn occurred at the beginning of the seventh century partly because of prior actions of the emperor Justinian. His brilliant jurist, Tribonion, in distilling the ancient Roman law created the legal system enabling the little horn's rise to power. In the third edition of *The Institutes of Roman Law,* Rudolf Sohm refers to the work assigned to Tribonian by Justinian: "No matter now whether the Roman State perished or not, Roman law was strong enough to survive the Roman Empire." The mean date of this law's origin—the mean of the year when it was commenced and when it was completed—is significant as the beginning of one of Daniel's time, times and half a time, or 1,260 years (527 start date + 534 completion date, divided by 2 = 531, rounded off.) Clearly the Roman state was legal Rome. The law that survived was the real sinew or life of the Roman Empire. Thus the Roman Empire actually survived its fall via survival of the Roman law. It empowered the little horn! Justinian's code became the legal setting for Medieval Europe, a Europe controlled by the Roman bishop, and formed the juridical matrix in which the old Roman Empire could be reborn in a politicized, essentially totalitarian religion. The sorely wounded beast would soon come alive again! Incidentally Dr. Schofield sees the sore wounding as the end of political Rome only.

We are witnessing the solidification of a dichotomous entanglement, the total politicization and state control of Christianity coupled with church control of the state or at least of the citizens of the state, helpless to do anything about it. In a letter to the Roman bishop dated March 533 A.D., Justinian writes: "We suffer not anything that belongs to the state of the churches to be done without submitting it to your holiness, who art head of all the churches." Was this not a strong prelude to the final creation of absolute power over western Christendom by the Bishop of Rome? This letter was incorporated into the civil law! Johannes II was Bishop of Rome at this time, but the communication appears to confirm a verbal commitment made to Boniface II in the year 531.

> Justinian, says the greatest English legal authority on his work, Mr. [James] Bryce, 'probably never dreamt of the dangerous consequences which might follow the exemptions from civil jurisdiction which he conceded to the clergy, and the large powers of administering not only ecclesiastical but charitable property which he conferred upon the bishop [of Rome].' (Hutton, *The Church of the Sixth Century*, 28)

In *The Decline and Fall of the Roman Empire*, Gibbon writes:

By the oppressive laws of Justinian the adversaries of the church were made the enemies of the state. ... It affords an unfavorable prejudice that his theology should form a very prominent feature of his portrait. ... His Code, and even more especially his Novels, confirm and enlarge the privileges of the clergy; and in every dispute between a monk and a layman, the partial judge was inclined to pronounce that truth and innocence and justice were always on the side of the church. (P. 1535)

The Reverend George Stanley Faber, B.D., adds:

About the year 533 or 534 the emperor Justinian declared the Pope to *Head of all the Churches.* ... No authority was then given into the hand of the little horn. ... No authority was then given to the Bishop of Rome which at all corresponds with the idea of *universal episcopacy.* Phocas [Western Roman Empire emperor] declared the Pope [71 years later] to be at once *head of all the churches,* which is a title of precedence and dignity and sole *universal Bishop* which is a title of authority, because he forbade all the other patriarchs to assume it: whereas although Justinian conferred upon him the first of these titles, yet at the very same time he styled the Patriarchy of Constantinople *Head of all the other churches.* A comparison is accordingly drawn very judiciously by Brightman between the grant of Justinian and the grant of Phocas in which he states that the former merely gave the Pope precedence of all his Episcopal brethren, but that the latter exclusively constituted him *universal Bishop*, assigning to him the whole world for his diocese. That this was really the case, any person may satisfy himself by consulting the Noveallae [a part of the ecclesias-

tical division of Justinian's, or Tribonian's, distilled
Roman law]. (*The Time of the End*, 75–76)

Thus the legal power, the ultimate power, of the little horn
was established in the era of 529 to 533, and the mean average
of those dates is the year 531 A.D. However important the law,
Daniel's little horn also needed a state from which to rule. In *The
Church of the Sixth Century*, Hutton writes that "the victories of
Justinian's armies gave back a mighty heritage to the empire.
Once more the Caesar ruled at Rome and at Ravenna, and the
Catholic Church held sway at Cordova and at Carthage" (15).

Historians of the period credit the Roman bishop with aiding
the emperor's efforts at this period (see *On the Four Prophetic
Empires*, 192–193). As Lord points out, this overthrow of the
nonorthodox Vandal of Geilomie, of the nonorthodox Ostrogoth
regime of Witigis and finally of the nonorthodox Ostrogoth
regime of Tortilla, were the three horns of Daniel to be removed
so that the little horn could essentially exert the power of Rome.

Of Justinian's distilled Roman law, J.B. Bury writes that "the
Code, Digest and Institutions form the principle parts of the
Corpus Juris Civilis, on which the law of most European coun-
tries is based, and which influenced English law, although it was
never accepted in England [emphasis added]" (*History of the Later
Roman Empire*, 399). Bury also writes, "Of Justinian one great
living authority has said 'No Roman emperor so nearly assumed
the position of a temporal Pope,' and another has described the
ecclesiastical history of the reign under the title of 'Justinian's
Caesaropapism.'"

The term "pragmatic sanction," meaning essentially the arbitrary rule by the will of the emperor, is referred to frequently in
writing about this period. The significance of all this to the subject at hand is that Justinian was essentially a theologian and set
in motion, because he had the power as emperor, the little horn's
reign or power. Justinian's restoration of the Western Roman
Empire was a direct result of the downfall of the three kingdoms
mentioned above, or the downfall of the three horns referred to
in Daniel. Clearly, without the existence of a Roman political

empire there could be no evolution into a Roman ecclesiastical empire, the empire of the little horn.

J.B. Bury writes:

> The Pragmatic Sanction or expression of the will of the sovereign was how Justinian ruled Italy after overthrowing the three sovereigns, especially the Ostrogoth. ... Justinian asserted the principle that doctrinal decisions could be made by imperial edicts. In 554 the Emperor issued his solemn Pragmatic Sanction for the government of Italy. Of this, section XII, gives a power to the bishops, which shows the intimate connection between State and Church. Justinian's new administration of Italy was to be military, but hardly less was it to be ecclesiastical. This rule of the Pragmatic Sanction was not an isolated instance; at every point the bishop [of Rome] was placed in rapport with the State. ...
>
> At the beginning of the sixth century not the pope, but Theodoric was master of Rome. ... The end of the sixth century showed that power would return in the end to the city which had founded the Empire, and to the Church which was now claiming to teach and to unite the nations." (*History of the Later Roman Empire*)

Schaff writes:

> The rise of Christianity was accompanied by a remarkable series of persecutions of heresies. ... When he [Justinian] supported the catholic, the universal faith, he was supporting the universal empire, the Roman world-state. The centre of this Catholicism was Rome, the ancient capital of the empire, and still its moral leader ... with penal laws against every departure from the orthodox Catholic creed, which was recognized and pro-

tected as the only religion of the state. ... Thus Rome, substituting the law for the sword, ruled the world once more for centuries and subdued the descendants of the very barbarians who had destroyed her [secular] empire. In the words of Dean Milman (Book III, Chapter 5), ... "The ancient Roman theory, that the religion of the state must be the religion of the people, which Christianity had broken to pieces by its inflexible resistance, was restored in more than its former rigor." (*History of the Christian Church*)

So we see that Tribonian's distillation of the ancient Roman law under Emperor Justinian became in effect an ecclesiastic compilation to enforce the authority of the Bishop of Rome down through the ages and governed Europe down the centuries to modern times; although its ecclesiastic power has now waned, Luther's Reformation weakened obedience to its authority to some extent in Europe, while England and the United States never accepted it. The Justinian legal system could hardly have been more the antithesis of a law "of the people, by the people and for the people." This latter concept of law was an absolute prerequisite for the permanent establishment of the nation destined to shepherd the Second Advent until it should ultimately destroy the "atheism of matter" and release all mankind from sin, sickness, and death. Jesus assured mankind that it would "lead into all truth" and that it would be as a baker woman "hiding a leaven in three measures of meal." Does this leaven affect the entire meal of adamantine human belief until it, in Paul's "twinkling of an eye," destroys irreversibly the Adamic mass of sin, sickness, and death? The Christian Science church is legally protected by the blessed laws of this nation and particularly by its Bill of Rights amendments. This nation will therefore survive until the fulfillment of all things.

To repeat Pagels: "Yet, as we have seen, Christians during the first centuries would not have imagined that their vision of a society characterized by liberty and justice could be the basis for a political agenda. ... Centuries, even millennia, would pass before such visions began to inform actual political aspirations and institutions: and only the most optimistic among us may still hope that such visions will one day achieve political reality" (*Adam, Eve and the Serpent,* 149). Such vision will come about only when the acceptance of Christian Science becomes more widespread. Again, there is a step beyond Pagels's vision. Following the realization of her vision is the total redemption of mankind from "the atheism of matter." Christian Science shows that matter is at best an adamantine existence and that when in fact we awake from this material illusion we will see that there is and ever has been only *one* existence, one reality, and this one totally spiritual. Eddy writes in *Science and Health:* "In the midst of imperfection, perfection is seen and acknowledged only by degrees. The ages must slowly work up to perfection. How long it must be before we arrive at the demonstration of scientific being, no man knoweth,—not even 'the Son but the Father,' but the false claim of error continues until the goal of goodness is assiduously earned and won" (233).

Schaff writes in *History of the Christian Church:* "The Justinian Code [527–534, the mean date being $527+534/2=531$] transmitted to the Middle Ages the legislative wisdom and experience of republican and imperial Rome at the same time with penal laws against every departure from the orthodox Latin creed, which was recognized and protected as the only religion of the state."

Schaff also writes that the "Common Law, the unwritten traditional law of England and America, though descending from the Anglo–Saxon times, therefore from heathen Germandom has ripened under the influence of Christianity and the church, and betrays this influence even far more plainly than the Roman Code, especially in all that regards the individual and personal rights and liberties of man" (111).

Bill of Rights
2

Catherine Drinker Bowen introduces her book *Miracle in Philadelphia* with the following words: "Miracles do not occur at random, nor was it the author of this book who said there was a miracle at Philadelphia in the year 1787. George Washington said it, and James Madison" (vii). In the introduction to *Miracle in Philadelphia*, Henry Steel Commager writes, "Americans were the first people in recorded history to 'bring forth' a new nation and the first, too, to found it upon a central body of Principles, which they set forth in the preamble to their Declaration of Independence and then in the preamble to their Constitution." On this topic, Margaret Thatcher said, "Europe was created by history, America was created by philosophy." During the period of the Constitutional Convention, James Madison said, "Every word of [the Constitution] decides a question between power and liberty." Commager said the words of the Constitution "were steeped, too, in the political theology of the British Puritans" and cited The *Pennsylvania Journal* as writing, "All the fortunes of the future are involved in this momentous undertaking." William Gladstone called the document "the most wonderful work ever struck off at a given time by the brain and purpose of man." Commager said, "Those who declared independence and wrote the Constitution did not originate these principles; they were rooted in classical history and philosophy, in *Puritan theology* [emphasis added]."

Such a background of informed opinion justifies Commager's evaluation: "The Constitution ... was an expression of political genius comparable in its intellectual distinction to the works of artistic genius in Renaissance Florence, of literary genius in Elizabethan England, and of musical genius in the eighteenth century Germanys."

The X factor giving the Constitution its immortal nature was the incorporation of Puritan theology into it. Puritanism nurtured the baker woman in her early upbringing. Jefferson opined that this Republic was based on Judeo–Christianity and that if we lose this, we will *ipso facto* lose the Republic. Can it be any wonder that a document of the above accolades should have been predicted by Daniel's Scriptural arithmology? A careful consideration of these and other similar academic accolades compared with Justinian's distilled Roman law reveals this remarkable Constitution as precisely antidotal to the centuries-old mischief perpetrated by this inquisitionist Roman law. This remedial process, as has been discussed earlier in this work, follows Daniel's Scriptural arithmology. First occurs historical events falling into the category of what the authorized Scripture (King James) refers to as an "abominable desolation." Then follow corrective events after so many of Daniel's prophetic times (1,260 years, 1,290 years, and 1,305 years). In this case, it took 1,260 prophetic years. The document might not be perfect, but it is the clarion call, sounding down the ages, man's inalienable rights. With respect to lack of perfection, Benjamin Rush, the distinguished Philadelphia surgeon who signed the Declaration of Independence, appeared before the Amendment Committee, imploring them to add a freedom of medical choice to the Bill of Rights. He cautioned them that the arrogance of his profession would grow into such prestige and power that eventually it would be accepted as the authority on medicine. He felt strongly and keenly that no such authority should exist and that it would be invasive on the individual rights of people not embracing the hosts of Aesculapius. His prediction has not been found wanting.

Eddy writes in *Science and Health*: "In the midst of imperfection, perfection is seen and acknowledged only by degrees. The ages must slowly work up to perfection. How long it must be before we arrive at the demonstration of scientific being, no man knoweth,—not even 'the Son but the Father,' but the false claim of error continues until the goal of goodness is assiduously earned and won" (233).

Birth of Mary Baker Eddy
3

According to Genesis 1:15, "God made two great lights; the greater light to rule the day, and the lesser light to rule the night."

Light here is the Hebrew word *ma'ar* and means a feminine luminary. In his King James Bible reference edition, C.I. Schofield says, "The greater light is a type of the Christ. ... He will take this character at his Second Advent" (4). The year 1821 gave birth to the woman God crowned and who was destined to write the book with the key to the Scriptures, which when unlocked would lead into all truth, as Jesus had promised when he spoke of the messenger bearing the "spirit of truth." The year 1821 was a remarkable year, freighted as it was with significant world events that in themselves were hints of things to come. This was the year Champollion deciphered Egyptian hieroglyphics using the Rosetta stone, thus unlocking with that key the ancient mysteries of Egypt. Faraday unlocked the mystery of electromagnetic rotation, which had a profound impact on modern society and its dependency upon electromagnetic generation of electricity. No household today could do without it. No industry or institution could do without it. Herman von Helmholtz, the great German physicist, was born. His contribution to our modern scientific age is incalculable. He unlocked some of the deep problems of physics. T.J. Seebeck unlocked the secrets of thermoelectricity. Sir Charles Wheatstone unlocked many hidden electrical methods and demonstrated sound reproduction.

Would it be much of an exaggeration to designate the year 1821 as a year pointing to the phenomena of discovery or "unlocking," either in the form of the actual discoveries or in the form of the birthdays of those who would be the discoverers?

Again the atmospheric zeitgeist was ripe for the birth appearance of those destined to produce such phenomena.

Discovery of Christian Science

4

In 1875, Mary Baker Eddy wrote *Science and Health with Key to the Scriptures*. She describes herself as being "a scribe under orders." She never claimed personal credit for a single word in that remarkable volume! This book became the textbook of her 1866 discovery of Christian Science—a discovery she attributes to divine influence. The decade following 1865 to 1866 had profoundly important discoveries. They pointed in a significant way to seminal changes of human thought. Indeed, thought experienced a paradigm change in direction, but all in accordance with Daniel 12:4, in which we read, "But thou, O Daniel, shut up the words and seal the book, even to the time of the end: many shall run to and fro, and *knowledge* [emphasis added] shall be increased." Perhaps the most profound and far-reaching change in knowledge came in the form of mathematics. In 1875 George Ferdinand Ludwig Phillip Cantor was completing his work on transfinite numbers that he patented in 1876. For centuries mathematicians had been struggling with the mathematical concept of infinity but with little or no success. Mathematicians, like all of us, had been "locked in" such a finite sense of things that they thought that if one removed an amount of anything from something, that something would thereafter be lessened by the amount removed. Cantor's set theory showed mathematically that this was not necessarily so. He was able to demonstrate mathematically that *any* quantity could be removed from an infinite entity without diminishing that entity at all. One is reminded of the biblical story of the widow woman who kept filling vessels from a small vial of oil without diminishing the oil in the vial. Elijah, who understood that God's largess to us is unlimited or infinite, was thus able to prove Cantor's theory in the "real" world! In *Stories of Creation,* Ricardo Nirenberg wrote, "The mathematician George Cantor believed that his theory of transfinite numbers had been communicated to him from a 'more powerful energy.' A divine voice, like the angel who in old paintings whispers the Word to the Evangelist or the Translator, whispered to Cantor the Theorems of Ordered Sets. Don't smile. To anyone who has puzzled over old questions, Cantor's Set Theory opens vast and surprising views" (1). Another authority states, "Today Cantor's work is widely accepted by the mathematical community. His theory on infinite sets reset the foundation of nearly every mathematical field and brought mathematics to its modern form."

No wonder again that Daniel's Scriptural arithmology should penetrate into this era. This era saw the completion of the Atlantic

Cable in 1865. It saw the temple of scientific knowledge established in 1865, when the renowned Massachusetts Institute of Technology was founded. Alfred Nobel invented dynamite. James Clerk Maxwell did his brilliant work on electromagnetism. Three Nobel Prize winners were born. There were several instances of unusual "running to and fro." Perhaps the most interesting one was Edward Whymper's climbing the Matterhorn. This was perhaps the most significant beginning of the massive "running to and fro" of mankind. Daniel did not understand all of the significance of his vision of mankind's breaking-out of the age-old shackles. In fact, he literally said it gave him a headache.

All of the various historical facts mentioned above may at first glance appear irrelevant to the subject at hand. But in view of Daniel's linking these sorts of events with the main subject, their actual historical occurrence tend to further substantiate the correctness of his vision of the main subject, and since he linked them together, it seems proper for the writer to do so.

As for prophecy, according to *The Time of the End*, published in 1856, "It is a singular fact in the history of Prophetic Interpretation that, in a majority of instances, the calculations of those who have attempted to penetrate the mystery of the Prophetic Periods have looked with interest to various epochs within the half-century extending from 1830 to 1880" (48). This book also states: "… David Parcus, D.D., who was born in Silesia in 1518, and commenced the 1,260 years in 605. This would terminate them in 1865, or 6,—a point within" (65). David Pareuw, who presided over the Academy of Heidelberg, delivered an address in 1608 with the date 1866 fixed for the Second Advent. Professor William Whiston, A.M., successor of Sir Isaac Newton in the Mathematical Professorship at Cambridge, also dates 1866. Four or so additional divines of hundreds of years ago also predict 1866. Some predict 1875, which is the year Eddy authored the textbook of her 1866 discovery, *Science and Health with Key to the Scriptures.*

The words of the immortal Isaac Newton may again be considered: "As the few and obscure prophecies concerning Christ's *first* [emphasis added] coming were for setting up the Christian religion, which all nations have since corrupted; so, the many and clear prophecies concerning the things to be done at His second coming are not only for predicting, but also for effecting, a *recovery* [emphasis added] and establishment of the long-lost truth, and setting up a kingdom wherein dwelleth righteousness" (*The Time of the End*, 314). This is the mission of the Second Coming, the 1866 discovery of Christian Science, and it is verily "effecting a recovery and establishment of the long-lost truth, and setting up a kingdom wherein dwelleth righteousness." Jesus prophesied that this "Second Coming" would "lead into *all* [emphasis added] truth." Hence the Christian Science textbook contains the *Science* of the Christ, and this time it will never be lost to the ages again. In the early Christian era, the disciples were simply not ready for the science of Jesus' teaching. Indeed, even short of the total Science of Christ, he said to them, "I have many things to tell you, but you cannot hear [understand] them now."

With all due respect to the brilliant genius Stephen Hawking and his colleagues, it is a shame that they apparently have little interest in biblical topics that held the attention of their equally brilliant, world-renowned Cambridge predecessors! Even their theories *hint* of something more profound than gross materialism! If matter is substance and there was no matter preceding the big bang, and if the big bang's very existence started with nothing more than a mathematical equation or, even worse, human postulation, then it would appear to follow that the cosmic model evolved from the big bang is postulation, however consistent with observation! This points again to J.S. Haldane's conclusion that "materialism, once a scientific theory is now the fatalistic creed of thousands, but materialism is nothing better than superstition on the same level as belief in witches and devils." The big bang itself is a type of witch, a creature of speculation who creates something out of nothing! Matter itself may be a type of misconception or misinterpretation of the substance of that which is.

Christian Science is healing the sick, reforming the sinner, in the way Jesus did it. It is lifting its students into the unlimited possibilities of thought released from material finite premises and conclusions. It is showing *how* Jesus could feed thousands with a few fishes and have twelve baskets full left over. It will be the ultimate destroyer of "the atheism of matter," the adamantine conviction of the human mind. Its more advanced demonstrations are yet to come but it is now restoring the sick and the sinning, healing relationships, comforting the mourners as only a true understanding of the Christ can, supplying God's provender where there is great need, and restoring hope to the hopeless in a thorough manner as only some understanding of the Science of the Christ can do. This is the "bread" resulting from the three measures of meal the Master referred to concerning the female baker, the woman with the leaven. Since all of mankind's thinking and experience is embraced in some combination of his scientific beliefs, his medical beliefs and his theological beliefs would these not be the *three* measures of meal that our beloved Master prophesied would be leavened? Would not this leavening be the correction of all that is wrong in human theory and thus release mankind from being the bonded servant held in the adamantine yoke of false human concepts? The true science would certainly be the truth and our Master said, "Ye shall know the truth and the truth shall make you free." The unleavened bread of ancient theology will be exchanged for the "bread which cometh down from heaven" and this bread is not unleavened! But it took centuries for mankind to mature enough to be ready for leavened bread for until "the fullness of time," mankind, to use Jesus' words, could not hear the deeper meaning. He could not digest leavened bread.

Fourth Abomination Period

❶

Dejure Status of Bishop of Rome

During this period the emperor Phocas bestowed upon the Bishop of Rome the legal status of "head" or "leader" of all clergy" including the other bishops. This act gave Legal status to the *little horn*. The *little horn* was now coalescing with single source authority. And now one individual embodied the incredible clerical power bestowed by Justinian's distilled Roman law! In time the *little horn* would cause the Roman Empire to be known in history as *THE HOLY ROMAN EMPIRE.* The student of history should himself judge how "holy" it was. Mankind was entangled in the adamantine clutches of matter, like Pegasus, with no theology which could liberate him. Our Master said: "Beware the leaven [theology] of the Scribes and Pharisees." The scribes and Pharisees showed mankind what the clergy, with absolute power over its people, can do! The next 600 years or so from this date many historians consider being the darkest period in human *history.* Interestingly Jesus said, "work while it is day for the night cometh when no man can work." By now Christian healing had yielded to the Roman *materia medica* of ancient pagan Greece and is still holding fast. Jesus' first command was "heal the sick." It is self-evident he meant for us to heal the way he did it-not Aesculapian.

❷

Discoverer

On this date Mary Baker Eddy experienced a serious accident on a slippery sidewalk in Lynn Massachusetts. The accident was considered fatal by the physician in attendance and her burial clothes were prepared. She reached for her Bible, had a profound answer to prayer, and was healed. In her words from *Science and Health With Key to the Scriptures:* "When apparently near the confines of mortal existence, standing already within the shadow of the death-valley, I learned these truths in divine Science: . . .".

But it was not in any sense an unprepared-for-insight. She had been praying and searching the Scriptures for years in search of what lay behind the works of her beloved Christ Jesus whom she had been especially taught since childhood to love. And in the preceding years to this date she had performed some remarkable healings herself. But she had been striving and praying in her Bible studies to know the Science behind the Christian healing phenomenon. She was convinced that it was somehow God's "law" and not a "miracle" that accounted for Jesus' remarkable achievements. This date marks the discovery, the culminating insight, of her long search, Scriptural study and unceasing prayer to God. In her own words, "God had been graciously preparing me during many years for this final discovery." Her heartfelt desire for that which would ultimately free all mankind from what she referred to as "the atheism of matter" would lead forward from here. She nominated her discovery Christian Science.

❸

Founder

The founding date of the Christian Science permanent church organization under the *Manual of the Mother Church* written by Mary Baker Eddy.

❹

Leader

Mary Baker Eddy officially recognized by her Church, after much detailed research into her private writings, as fulfilling the Scriptural prophecy of "the woman God crowned" (Revelation 12:1 thus officially establishing her as "the crowned one" or Permanent Leader of the Cause prophesied by Jesus also in Matthew 13:33 and in John 16:13. The year 1941 is the mean of the year 1938 when the research began and the year 1943, when the results were published

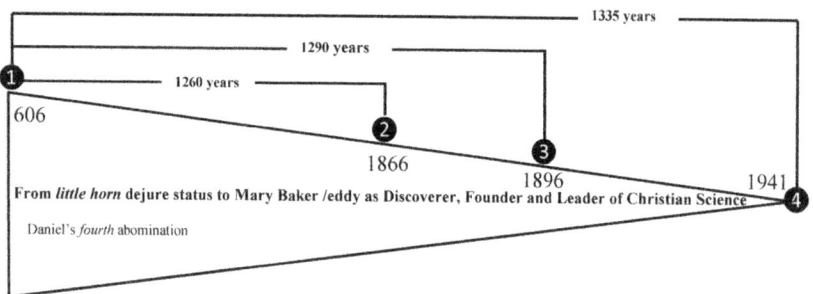

From *little horn* dejure status to Mary Baker /eddy as Discoverer, Founder and Leader of Christian Science

Daniel's *fourth* abomination

Figure 7

Chapter V
From Frederic the Great and Little Horn De jure Status to Mary Baker Eddy as Discoverer, Founder, and Leader of Christian Science

De jure Status of Little Horn
1

The emperor Phocas (602 to 610) was the first emperor to bestow *de jure* power upon the Bishop of Rome. Although the distilled Roman law of Justinian had bestowed incredible legal power upon the Bishop of Rome, he had not yet been endowed with *de facto legal* recognition as the absolute head of *all* bishops, especially the bishop of Constantinople. Phocas was not highly regarded as an emperor by such scholars as J.B. Bury. Pernice and Sprinter favored him no better. According to these scholars, he was a "shapeless monster" and "the most perverse and ferocious tyrant that ever donned the imperial diadem." The emperor's bestowal clearly was an important link in the chain that held mankind in the jaws of the Roman beast after the little horn had turned Rome into ecclesiastical despotism.

Sabinianus was elected Bishop of Rome on September 13, 594, and deceased February 22, 606. This date marked the death of the last Bishop of Rome not invested with the title of pope and who was considered equal to the other bishops throughout

Christendom, but not superior to them. In other words, he had
no papal supremacy and was no vicegerent of God. The next
bishop, Boniface III, was on the seat of the Roman bishopric
from February 19, 607, through November 12, 607. Schaff, in
the *History of the Christian Church,* says that he "did not scruple
to assume the title of 'universal bishop,' against which Gregory I
in proud humility had so indignantly protested as a blasphemous
antichristian assumption."

The eleventh edition of *Encyclopedia Britannica* says:

> With the decay of the empire the title [Pontific
> Maximus] very naturally fell to the Popes, whose
> function as administrators of religious law closely
> resembled those of the ancient Roman [pagan]
> priesthood, hence the modern use of "Pontiff" and
> "Pontifical."
>
> Growing up under the shadow of the Empire,
> the Church too became an empire, as the Empire
> had become a church. As it took over something of
> the old pagan ceremonial, so it took over much of
> the old secular organization. The pope borrowed
> his title of *pontifax maximus* from the emperor:
> What is far more, he made himself gradually, and
> in the course of centuries, the Caesar and
> Imperator of the Church. The offices and the dio-
> ceses of the Diocletian empire: the whole spirit of
> orderly hierarchy and regular organization, which
> breathes in the Roman Church, is the heritage of
> ancient Rome. (s.v. "Empire")

Most scholars opine that by this time, Pope Gregory had quite
well consolidated the ultimately total power of the papacy.
Despite his various disavowals, he certainly had carried the
papacy to supreme heights.

"Boniface the Third was created Pope on the 15th of February,
in the year 606. His accession took place in the midst of a quarrel
between the emperor Phocas and the Patriarch of Constantinople;
the result of which was that Phocas forbade the Patriarch to style

himself 'Universal Bishop,' and conferred that name *exclusively* [emphasis added] on the Roman Pontiff" (Schaff, *History of the Christian Church*, 607).

In *Time of the End,* the Rev. George Stanley Faber wrote, "Let it be noted that this Roman emperor removed all claim of any other Bishop to any kind of papal title" (70). This time there was no *almost*.

Now with total power in his hands, the little horn afterward created a history of incredible persecutions, inquisitions, and deprivation of rights of conscience, causing such persons as Galileo to shame themselves from fear of the car of the inquisition, and, executing such worthies as Savonarola. According to John Foxe's *Book of Martyrs,* the Dark Ages following this era saw over sixty million people put to death directly or indirectly under the tyranny of the little horn. Scholars consider the next six hundred or so years to be the darkest era in human history. The Rev. John Cox's insight is especially revealing:

> Paganism had re-entered, whole and entire, into the religion which seemed to have annihilated it. The Christian religion, which might on several accounts have been accused already of turning back towards Polytheism [Nicaean Council's trinity theory?], found itself changed, by a last step, into idolatry properly so called. The images, the statues, were recognized as having in their very nature something divine. They were honored for themselves, independent of the object they represented, more perhaps than had even been done among the pagans. ... The Moslems lavished on the Christians the reproach of idolatry; they turned against them all the arguments which the ancient apologists had used to attack the pagans; and this controversy was so much the more humiliating for the orthodox as their profession of faith formed an evident contrast with their practice; and the hatred of the name idolater, was not extinct in them. At the very time

when they most richly deserved it. (*On the Four
Prophetic Empires*, 165)

The emperor Phocas put the finishing touches on the power
of the little horn. For more than a millennia and a half hence, the
ancient Roman Empire, under its new ecclesiastical form, was to
rule the conscience of mankind. Only a new type of religious leadership could lead mankind out of this morass, but it could never
happen under the old Roman environment. The zeitgeist for such
cannot be found there. Ecclesiastical Rome experienced religious
intolerance of historical magnitude coupled in the year 606 with
de jure power to enforce it! The old Roman mandate of absolute
control had simply evolved from the political into the ecclesiastical in direct fulfillment of Daniel's prophecy.

Gibbon writes of Gregory: "The celestial honours have been
liberally bestowed by the authority of the Popes, but Gregory is
the last of their own order whom they have presumed to inscribe
in the calendar of saints" (Gibbon, *Decline and Fall*, 755). This
Roman bishop brought the power of the little horn into its
height, and soon after the emperor bestowed upon it its *de jure*
status. Phocas had for a long time been under the influence of
Gregory. Gibbon writes: "Their temporal power insensibly arose
from the calamities of the times; and the Roman bishops, who
have deluged Europe and Asia with blood, were compelled to
reign as the ministry of charity and peace" (ibid., 755).

The distinguished eleventh edition of the *Encyclopedia
Britannica* says of Gregory:

> For the *first* [emphasis added] time in history
> the pope appeared as a political power, a temporal
> prince. He appointed governors to cities, issued
> orders to generals, provided munitions of war, sent
> his ambassadors to negotiate with the Lombard
> king and actually dared to conclude a private peace.
> In this direction Gregory went farther than any of
> his predecessors: he laid the formations of a polit-
> ical influence which endured for centuries. (s.v.
> "Popes")

What Phocas did in 606 merely formalized the Gregory achievement! Of the medieval papacy, says Henry Hart Milman:

> The real father is Gregory the Great. In respect of the methods of conversion which he advocated he was not less intolerant than his contemporaries. In respect of his character, while most historians agree that he was a really great man, some deny that he was also a great saint. The worst blot on his fair fame is his adulatory congratulation of the murderous usurper Phocas. (Ibid., s.v. "Popes")

Milman, a great Oxford historian of Latin Christianity writes in *History of Latin Theology* (1860):

> Of the medieval papacy, the real father is Gregory the Great. The pragmatic sanction (554), promulgating the Justinian Code, separated the civil from the military power, and, by conferring on the bishops the authority over the provincial and municipal government, soon led to the increase of the power of the Church. In Rome we behold the rapid growth of the papal power and the continued increase of its political influence. ... Meanwhile the Roman episcopate developed into the papacy, which claimed supremacy over the entire Christian church, and actually exercised it increasingly in the west from the fifth century on. (P. 44)

Gregory's years of influence on Phocas no doubt entered into Phocas's decision to grant *de jure* status to the Bishop of Rome. With this significant act, the year 606 saw the *completion* of the little horn prototype represented by Gregory, for this was the year Phocas gave *de jure* recognition to Pope Boniface III and hence to the institution of the papacy. This event occurred only two years after Gregory's death. This bestowal upon Pope Boniface endured as a permanent thread interwoven into the garment of the papacy.

If Milman is correct and the real father of the medieval papacy is Gregory, then Gregory personifies the little horn in his final developed form.

From the third volume of *History of the Christian Church*, Schaff writes that "with Gregory I (590–604) a new period begins. Next to Leo I, he was the greatest of the ancient bishops of Rome, and he marks the transition of the patriarchal system into the strict papacy of the middle ages. For several reasons we prefer to place him at the head of the succeeding period. ... He even solemnly protested ... against the title of *universal bishop* ... He declared it an *antichristian* assumption. .,, When we take his operations in general into view and remember the rigid consistency of the papacy, which never forgets, we are almost justified in thinking, that this protest was directed not so much against the title itself, as against the bearer of it and proceeded more from jealousy of a rival at Constantinople, than from sincere humility."

The action of Phocas just a few short years later tends to support this opinion. Phocas was greatly influenced by the views of Gregory.

Discoverer
2

Obviously, the Science of the Christ had always been here. Jesus practiced it hourly. Eddy could not let go of the conviction that the works of her beloved Savior were indeed the outcome of his natural ability to grasp overwhelmingly a sensibility that God's power is not only omnipotent but *natural*. This conviction immediately ruled out of her thought the traditional conception that miracles were involved. In every case, his remarkable works were the result of God's *law*. Quite clearly, by the very definition of *miracle,* anything governed by law is not a miracle. She realized that his virgin conception brought forth a man largely free from the absolute conviction that man is a sensuous machine constructed out of flesh and blood. This, then, must mean that scientific law lay behind his remarkable career. She *must* know the Science of these laws. She realized that scientific law manifests scientific principle, and this led to her remarkable realization that in addition to God's other "names," He must be recognized also as divine Principle.

That fortuitous day in Lynn, Massachusetts, in the year 1866, when her near-fatal accident was removed from history by a profound realization that no such thing could happen in the kingdom of heaven, literally fulfilled that phrase from the Lord's Prayer, "Thy kingdom come." Are there accidents in God's kingdom? This Scientific proof set a permanent imprimatur upon mankind's future. It showed beyond cavil that divine power dominates the universe and that a realization of this will ultimately erase the adamantine conviction of material power and dominance. Thusly the kingdom of heaven is literally brought down to earth in the individual experience!

That remarkable day in Lynn was to set in motion a religious movement destined in time to liberate all mankind from the ravages of sin, sickness, and death.

Jesus said, "For as the lightning cometh out of the east and shineth even unto the west; so shall also the coming of the Son of man be." This is a prophecy that even as it first appeared in the near east, its Second Advent would be in the west. But this Second Advent would not, even as in the First Advent, at once restore the kingdom. The woman's leaven must first cause a change of base in human thinking and that would take time. Being based now on scientific understanding rather than on faith alone, this time there would be no interregnum of darkness as typified by Daniel's abominations.

In 1945 Irving Tomlinson wrote in *Twelve Years with Mary Baker Eddy:* "If the world is to receive the message of Christian *Science* [emphasis added] which Mrs. Eddy brought, then it must obtain a true estimate of the messenger. Christian Scientists are convinced that just as the advent of Jesus proved the 'first coming' of the Christ, so are they certain that Mary Baker Eddy's discovery of Christian Science fulfilled the prophecy of the 'second coming.' And there is ample biblical authority to substantiate the conviction that Mrs. Eddy was God's messenger to this age through whom the message of the 'second coming' was revealed to the world" (209). In the same work, he writes: "No one could serve twelve years under Mrs. Eddy's counsel and instruction without realizing how clearly she recognized her position as prophesied by St. John the Revelator ... for she perceived the fulfillment of the Revelator's prophecy in her own life, and in Christian Science. This is evidenced by her own words: 'The twelfth chapter of the Apocalypse, or Revelation of St. John, has a special suggestiveness in connection with the nineteenth century.' The real identity of God's messenger to this age will be unfolded as mankind seeks to understand it through a study of the Bible and her writings" (216–219).

In Jesus' parable, "the kingdom of heaven is like leaven which a woman took and hid in three measures of meal," the original was a leaven which *the* woman took, not *a* woman. Obviously, then, the Master was referring to a *particular* woman. Jesus' prophetic powers greatly exceeded that of the prophets, for they were able to prophesy with great accuracy the place and circumstances of Jesus' appearing as well as his suffering, but he even prophesied the very name of the woman with the leaven. The name "Baker" is hidden in the parable. No injustice is done to the passage to rephrase it, "The kingdom of heaven is like a leaven, which the Baker woman took and hid in three measures of meal till the whole was leavened." She was a baker woman both by virtue of maiden name and by the fact she was to leaven the bread of heaven as it was perceived before its science was revealed. Her leaven was destined to destroy the gods of materialism. Haldane has this to say about materialism: "Materialism, once a scientific theory is now the fatalistic creed of thousands, but materialism is nothing better than superstition on the same level as belief in witches and devils." In other words, it is belief in superstition. Until Jesus introduced the woman with the *leavened* bread, unleavened bread had heretofore in the Scriptures represented purity and righteousness. This kept superstition out of the Hebrew religion. Paul warned about these superstitions. Gnosticism and other special insights are examples of these impurities. The world was not yet ready for the *Science* of the Word! Leaven was needed in the bread of heaven, but it was only this kind of leaven that was needed. In the fullness of time, our heavenly Father supplied it. Eddy said that God had been preparing her for many years for this discovery of Christian Science. Thus she was predestined to become the discoverer of Christian Science, or the science of Christianity, and this was the nature of the Second Advent!

Although Eddy's discovery was congruent with her remarkable 1866 healing, it is of great interest to read in the preface of Eddy's Christian Science textbook, *Science and Health with Key to the Scriptures,* that as early as 1862 Eddy began to "write down and give to friends the results of her Scriptural study." Clinton, in his *Essay on Hebrew Chronology,* concludes in the third volume of his late, learned work, entitled *Fasti Hellenici,* that the opening of the Sixth seal of Revelation occurred in the year 1862. This date for the opening of the seventh millennium is concurred by other scholarly works, such as E.B. Elliott's *HorAE Apocalyptica.* In *Science and Health,* Eddy writes: "The twelfth chapter of the Apocalypse, or Revelation of St. John, has a special suggestiveness in connection with the nineteenth century. In the opening of the sixth seal, typical of six thousand years since Adam, the distinctive feature has reference to the present age" (559–560).

Founder

3

Following her remarkable discovery, Eddy performed many cases of divine healing, practicing the Science she had discovered. She also taught others this healing practice, and many remarkable healings were done by her and her students. But she realized that a textbook on this Science must be made available. In the year 1875, she published *Science and Health with Key to the Scriptures,* and this became the textbook of her teaching. However, she also realized that to perpetuate the teachings of Christian Science, an organization would be necessary. Over the next few years, an organization developed step-by-step until its final and permanent form evolved and its operations governed by the Church Manual. The final form became a *fait accompli* in the year 1896. Thus on this date, Mary Baker Eddy was established as the Founder of Christian Science.

The evolution of the church into its final form was accomplished through many events of both joyful and difficult struggles. Eddy was especially concerned that its established form could not be altered by human interference then or in the future. She knew what well-meaning, capricious human interference could do to an organization. As if in answer to prayer, she was led to a Massachusetts law relating to property and estates that was rather unique as such things go. This law virtually ensured an organization of such a legal status as to be essentially free from future human interference. Thus the church property and law of the Church Manual virtually guaranteed the future of her 1896 founding to be permanent.

The wisdom granted her by Providence has since been more than justified. Certain personages and organizations have in subsequent years attempted to interfere with the church operations because it did not please the way they wanted things to go. These things had been brought into court. In every case, the courts have ruled that these people and organizations had no legal standing because of the way the church was founded, and the cases were thrown out.

In addition to God's name as Principle, Eddy recognized Him also as Mind. Certainly it must have been the divine intelligence that guided her in this founding activity.

Daniel 8:11 says of the little horn that "by him the daily sacrifice was taken away ... and it cast down the truth to the ground." The daily sacrifice was, of course, the ritual sacrifice of animals. But this practice represented something much greater than mere animal sacrifice. It was, in fact, an acknowledgement of a power, a Truth higher than mere individuals. In the fullness of time, this would be no longer merely symbolic but would be clearly a sacrifice of the animal nature of man in recognition of his spiritual nature. Even the Old Testament rebukes the thought that very much is gained by the mere daily sacrifice of animals. In the Book of Leviticus, Moses sets out rather elaborate and complex rules for animal sacrifice and daily worship. The dominant element in all the ritual was *cleansing*. In an attempt to comprehend to some degree the overall significance of this complex ritual, the writer became convinced that the overall message was to instill purity of thought. Through an incredible sense of this state of thought, the Virgin ushered in the First Advent. The Mary of the Second Advent revealed the science of Jesus' teaching. This Science even cleansed the *supposed* existence of matter itself. Even natural science is beginning to suggest that this might be the case. After Einstein revealed it to be, at best, but a form of energy, who knows? The restoration of the daily sacrifice will ultimately lead to the realization that *all* is Spirit and spiritual, and God, Spirit, is indeed *all.* Throughout *Science and Health,* Eddy makes it clear that you cannot have it both ways.

The Word would never again degenerate through the mere leaven of the Scribes and Pharisees for the Holy Scriptures, and Science and Health were destined to be ordained as this church's only preachers. The sermons in this new Mother Church and in its branches throughout the world were to be read each Sunday by readers who would make no comment on the meaning but would let the Word speak for itself. The sermon for a given week would be studied each day by the membership prior to the Sunday services through a publication called the *Christian Science Quarterly.* Thus the daily sacrifice would be restored as predicted by Daniel—not by the sacrifice of animals, not symbolically, but in fact as a daily sacrifice of the animal qualities overcoming the erroneous belief that man is a statistically evolved animal molded out of matter. This process would gradually, through time, convince mankind that we are indeed in God's image and therefore are in no way animal or material, but truly spiritual beings right now. Through deep daily study and prayer over these Bible lessons, its adherents would spiritualize their thinking and purify their hearts, and in so doing, start lifting the burden of materialism off of all mankind. This daily sacrifice of self would ultimately bring in the millennium. Thus the daily sacrifice will have been restored on a far higher level than it had ever been before practiced or understood.

Eddy made clear that a major requirement of her church was to reinstate primitive Christian healing in direct obedience to the first command of Jesus of Nazareth. This art had been gradually lessening over three centuries until totally lost following the first Nicene Council. Greek or Aesculapian medicine, the medicine of the pagan Roman Empire, had replaced it.

Leader
4

Mary Baker Eddy's position as leader is essentially identical with her position as the baker woman with the three measures of meal prophesied by Jesus of Nazareth. A position statement concerning her leadership was published in *The Christian Science Journal* and the *Christian Science Sentinel* in 1943. The investigation leading to the report was commenced in 1938. Thus the mean date was $(1938 + 1943)/2 = 1940.5$, or 1941 rounded off.

> This position statement was based on the report of a six-member committee of editors and former editors of the Christian Science periodicals appointed by the Directors in April, 1938, to discover just what Mrs. Eddy believed concerning herself with respect to Scriptural prophecy. The committee was given access to Mrs. Eddy's private correspondence, as well as to her published writings. After prayerfully and carefully studying the evidence, this committee made a report to the Board of Directors of fifty-seven pages of typewritten evidence that Mrs. Eddy regarded herself as having fulfilled Bible prophecy. (Bliss Knapp, *The Destiny of the Mother Church,* [Boston: The Christian Science Publishing Society], 58)

The report on Eddy is repeated on page 58 of Knapp's *The Destiny of the Mother Church:*

Mrs. Eddy's Place

1. Mrs. Eddy, as the Discoverer and founder of Christian Science, understood herself to be the one

chosen of God to bring the promised Comforter to the world, and, therefore, the revelator of Christ, Truth, in this age.

2. Mrs. Eddy regarded portions of Revelation (that is, Chapter 12) as pointing to her as the one who fulfilled prophecy by giving the full and final revelation of Truth; her work thus being complementary to that of Christ Jesus.

3. As Christ Jesus exemplified the fatherhood of God, she (Mrs. Eddy) revealed God's motherhood; she represents in this age the spiritual idea of God typified by the woman in the Apocalypse. [See *Science and Health*, 565]

4. Mrs. Eddy considered herself to be the "God-appointed" and "God-anointed" messenger to this age, the woman chosen by God to discover the Science of Christian healing and to interpret it to Mankind; she is so closely related to Christian Science that a true sense of her is essential to the understanding of Christian Science, in other words, the revelator cannot be separated from the revelation.

5. This recognition of her true status enabled her to withstand the opposition directed against her by "the dragon" (malicious animal magnetism); she was touchingly grateful to those who saw her as the woman of prophecy and who therefore trusted, obeyed, and supported her in her mission.

6. This same recognition is equally vital to our movement, for demonstration is the result of vision; the collecting of this indisputable evidence of our Leader's own view of herself and of her mission marks a great step forward; wisely utilized, this ev-

idence will stimulate and stabilize the growth of Christian Scientists today and in succeeding generations; it will establish unity in the Field with regard to the vital question of our Leader's relation to Scriptural prophecy.

The concluding words were:

As we record these important facts, we remind Christian Scientists of our Leader's words, "The Scriptures and Christian Science reveal 'the way,' and personal revelators will take their proper place in history, but will not be deified."

Chapter VI
The Fall of the Four-Tiered Beast

The concatenated events developed in arrows 1–7 initiated the essential processes ultimately leading to the crashing of the stone of Figure 2 into the legs of all (including post-little horn) intrusion into the ultimate spiritual freedom of all mankind. This time the top-heavy man of Figure 1 will totally collapse. This is the time when the stone of Christian Science (the bedrock of the Christ) represented in Figure 2 will smash the legs of false human power, and the top-heavy beast will fall. This time represents the great discovery that is ultimately destined to destroy the adamantine illusion of life and intelligence in matter, the "time of the end" of matter as even an illusion. When the final full effects of the great discovery of Christian Science conquer *all* of human consciousness, the Spirit, which is God, will be the *only* substance cognized by man's consciousness. Mary Baker Eddy symbolizes Spirit by circles, spheres, and light because these helpful figures, unlike linear forms, have no beginning and no ending. Even as our Master used illustrations such as the mustard tree to get across an important point, so Eddy similarly used figures of speech, including geometric symbols. Take the following quote from *Science and Health*: "The real Life or Mind, and its opposite, the so-called material life and mind, are figured by two geometrical symbols, a circle or sphere and a straight line. The circle represents the infinite without beginning or end; the straight line represents the finite which has both beginning and end. The sphere represents good, the self-existent and eternal Individuality or Mind; the straight line represents evil, a belief in a self-made and temporary material existence. Eternal Mind and material existence never unite in figure or in fact" (282).

The river Hiddekel is mentioned only twice in the Bible, in the Book of Daniel and in the Book of Genesis. It is the biblical name for the river Tigris. Since it is one of the rivers flowing out of the Garden of Eden, the following is especially significant: In chapter 12, verse 5, Daniel writes of the river Hiddekel that there are three personages thereby. One is in the center of the river, and the other two are on each side of the river. Was the one in the center the Christ, and were the other two they who ushered in the Christ in the First and Second Advents? And did the flowing river represent the inexhaustible, ever-present God? The closing words of the Book of Daniel indicate that the river event will be significantly understood after the last abomination of desolation! The one in the center was asked a question. He replied that the scattering of the power of the holy people should occur for a time, times, and a half time, and then it would be over. This time constant (1,260 years) has been shown in this work to be the time interval between the most significant historic abuses (predicted by Daniel as to be abominable historic events unparalleled and inflicted upon the people of God yet to come, and the remarkable events to relieve such abuses). These 1,260 years apparently take on the character of a *social* numerical constant similar to the numerical constant π which relates strictly to *mathematical* matters. But if nature relates the sections of a circle with a mathematical constant, is it such a mental leap to suppose she might so relate human events? If this seems far-fetched, the reader's attention is called to the fact that recently mathematicians have discovered what appear to be numerical constants relating to human or social experiences.

The Baker woman says that "as a result of teaching Christian Science ethics and temperance have received an impulse, health has been restored, and longevity increased" (*Science and Health*, 348). She also comments from the Scripture: "The period required for this dream of material life, embracing its so-called pleasures and pains to vanish from consciousness 'knoweth no man, but the Father,' this period will be of longer or shorter duration according to the tenacity of error" (ibid., 77). But she is quite clear about what will accelerate the process. She says: "If all who seek his [Jesus'] commemoration through material symbols will take up the cross, heal the sick, cast out evils, and preach Christ, or Truth, to the poor,—the receptive thought,—they will bring in the millennium" (ibid., 34). As a matter of fact, longevity had been gradually decreasing since the early days preceding the patriarchs and reached its lowest level about the year 1866, the year Christian Science was discovered. Since that date it has steadily increased.

To repeat a previous quote, Pagels writes in *Adam, Eve, and the Serpent*: "Yet, as we have seen, Christians during the first centuries would not have imagined that their vision of a society characterized by liberty and justice could be the basis for a political agenda. ... Centuries, even millennium, would pass before such visions began to inform actual political aspirations and institutions; and only the most optimistic among us may still hope that such visions will one day achieve political reality" (55).

Such vision will come about only when the acceptance of Christian Science becomes more widespread. But it certainly will not happen under Augustine theology. But there is a step beyond Pagels's vision. Following the realization of her vision is the total redemption of mankind from "the atheism of matter." Christian Science shows that matter is at best an adamantine existence and that when in fact we awake from this material illusion, we will see that there is and ever has been only *one* existence and one reality, and this one totally spiritual.

Eddy writes in *Science and Health* (233) that "in the midst of imperfection, perfection is seen and acknowledged only by degrees. The ages must slowly work up to perfection. How long it must be before we arrive at the demonstration of scientific being, no man knoweth,—not even 'the Son but the Father,' but the false claim of error continues until the goal of goodness is assiduously earned and won."

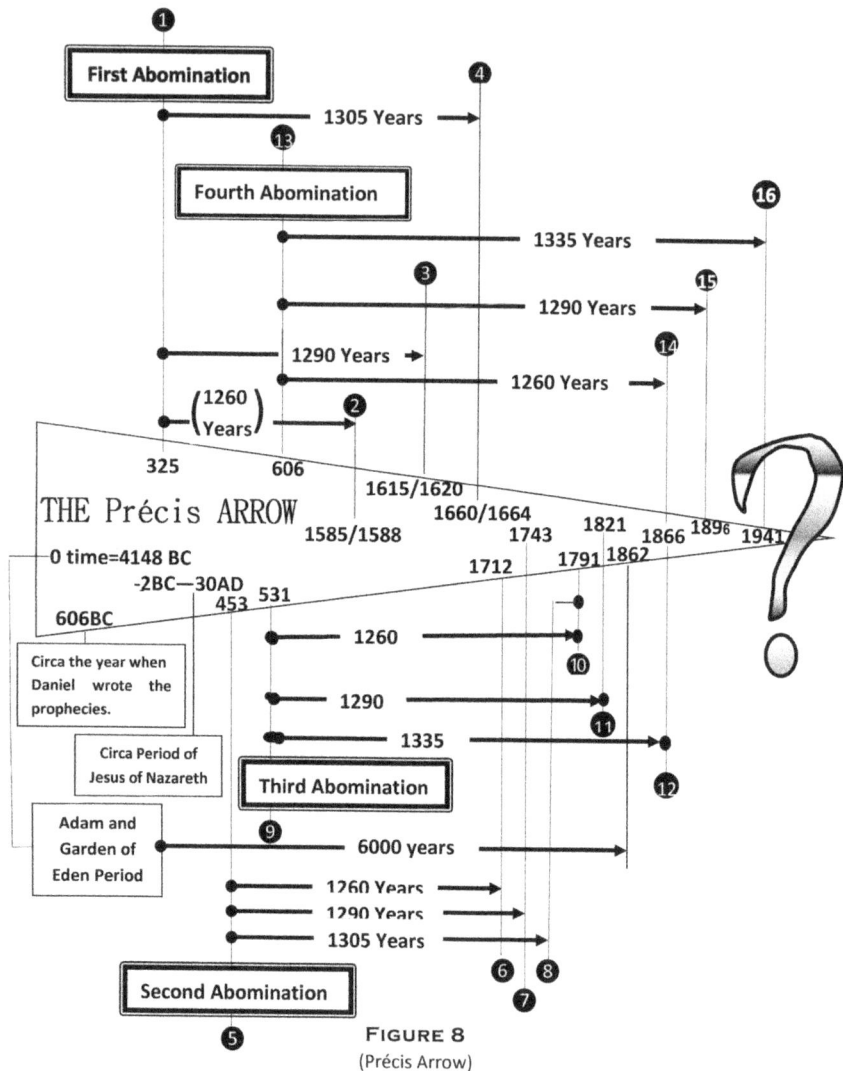

FIGURE 8
(Précis Arrow)

Chapter VII
Arrow Précis

The précis arrow is a combined summation of all the arrows in the text. It presents an overview that might by helpful in digesting the sum of all the arrows. There are some things about the arrow that might be more apparent in an overview.

If we consider Adam and the Garden of Eden experience of early mankind as 0 B.C., then the 6,000-year period terminates in 1862, according to Fenes Clinton, the nineteenth-century scholar, thinker, and writer on these matters, who wrote in his *Essay on Hebrew Chronology* that the year 1862 would end the six thousand years since Adam. Year "0," or the beginning date of time, would then occur in the year 4138 B.C.

Eddy writes in *Science and Health:* "As early as 1862 she began to write down and give to friends the results of her Scriptural study, for the Bible was her sole teacher." The sixth seal had been broken. The seventh millennium had arrived. This was the *beginning* of the period of the Second Advent.

Given Charles Darwin's theory of statistical evolution, the reader may be uncomfortable with the idea of setting an historical date as the beginning (the Garden of Eden commencing human history) equal to 0 followed by a 6,000-year span to the year 1862. But Darwin's theory is just that, a theory, and a theory without proof.

The distinguished mathematician Michael Guillen wrote in his excellent book *Bridges to Infinity*:

Controversial hypotheses (such as the Darwinian and teleological theories about the origin of our species) are widely accepted as true, even though they have not been *proved* [emphasis added] and perhaps never will be. ... In 1931 the mathematician's fantasy world became like the more realistic world when the Viennese logician Kurt Gödel proved that there will always be mathematical truths that cannot be proved with logic. Suddenly, there was introduced into the mathematical world a *formal* [emphasis added] role for *subjectivity* [emphasis added], since the *only* [emphasis added] possible way of avowing an unprovable truth, mathematical or *otherwise* [emphasis added] is to accept it as an article of faith. (P. 117)

As to the 6,000 years leading to 1862, Clinton was considered the expert in this field by the old Scriptural scholars who dealt with this sort of thing. In any case, if a Darwinian *material* world has any *substantial* reality, how was Jesus of Nazareth able to get into a boat on the Sea of Galilee and immediately it was on the other side? Albert Einstein might find this one fascinating!

Clinton gave years of his brilliant scholarship to the study of ancient Hebrew biblical and Hebrew Scriptural documents relating biblical events and their sequential periods of occurrence and thus developed a concatenated time flow! Thusly Clinton arrived at the conclusion that the year 1862 ushered in the Seventh Millennium.

First Abomination Period

That which started it all: The mandate of the emperor Constantine at the Council of Nicaea that the official religion of the Roman State would be the Christian religion and the subsequent introduction of polytheism into Christianity through that man-made theological doctrine known as the Trinity creed.

Christian healing, as Jesus taught it and gave to us as his *first* command, virtually disappeared after this council.

Second Abomination Period

Attila and Leo I: Due to pagan superstition, Attila the Hun was prevented from destroying Rome by the interference of Leo I, bishop of that city. Thus the very worst of all the pagans whose minds were set on destroying the *political* Roman Empire was unknowingly helping the establishment of *ecclesiastical,* or little horn, Rome. This event was a very important one in the development of little-horn control of western civilization until the coming of Martin Luther.

Third Abomination Period

Justinian's distilled Roman law: Justinian's brilliant Roman jurist, Tribonian, distilled the ancient Roman law and incorporated into it special privileges for the clergy, in effect handing over to the clergy virtual *legal* control of the religious conscience of the people. This set the stage for, and eventually led to, the emperor Phocas bestowing legal power to the Roman bishop exclusively. The little horn's power was completed by that act.

Fourth Abomination Period

Phocas: *De jure* power given to Roman Bishop: The "horn" of the little horn receives his full power with this act. This emperor had been clearly shaped and molded under the influence of Frederick the Great.

The question mark at the end of the précis arrow represents the question: When will the leavened bread of the Second Advent completely liberate mankind from the atheism of matter into his understanding of himself as God's image and likeness? Remember,

God is not matter. So how can His image and likeness be matter? Paul says that this moment will come in the twinkling of an eye. Jesus says that no man knoweth the hour, but the Father!

Nebuchadnezzar's Proclamation

Unto all people, nations, and languages, that dwell in all the earth; Peace be multiplied unto you. I thought it good to show the signs and wonders that the high God hath wrought toward me. How great is his signal! And how mighty are his wonders! His kingdom is an everlasting kingdom, and his dominion is from generation to generation. (Dan. 4:1–3)

FINIS